CALEB ROSS

Serverless API Development with Flask

Copyright © 2024 by Caleb Ross

All rights reserved. No part of this publication may be reproduced, stored or transmitted in any form or by any means, electronic, mechanical, photocopying, recording, scanning, or otherwise without written permission from the publisher. It is illegal to copy this book, post it to a website, or distribute it by any other means without permission.

First edition

This book was professionally typeset on Reedsy.
Find out more at reedsy.com

Contents

INTRODUCTION	1
Chapter 1: Getting Started with Flask and Serverless...	10
Chapter 2: Building and Deploying Your First Serverless...	22
Chapter 3: Scaling Flask APIs with AWS Lambda	33
Chapter 4: Securing Flask APIs in a Serverless Environment	43
Chapter 5: Optimizing Flask API Performance in a Serverless...	55
Chapter 6: Integrating Third-Party Services and APIs with...	85
Chapter 7: Testing Flask APIs: Strategies and Best Practices	98
Chapter 8: Deploying Flask APIs to Production	109
Chapter 8: Advanced Topics in Flask Development	120
Chapter 9: API Documentation: Best Practices and Tools	134
Chapter 10: API Versioning: Strategies and Best Practices	146
Chapter 11: Performance Optimization for Flask APIs	158
Chapter 12: Securing Your Flask API: Best Practices and...	183
Chapter 13: Effective API Documentation: Best Practices and...	199
Chapter 14: Managing API Deprecation and Sunset Policies	213
Chapter 15: API Testing and Monitoring: Ensuring Reliability...	222
Conclusion: The Future of API Development with Flask	233

INTRODUCTION

Introduction: The Power of Serverless with Flask

The landscape of web development and application programming interfaces (APIs) has drastically evolved over the past decade. With the rise of cloud computing, serverless architectures have emerged as a game-changer, allowing developers to focus solely on code, eliminating the need to manage or maintain underlying infrastructure. Flask, a micro web framework written in Python, pairs perfectly with serverless architectures due to its simplicity and flexibility. This combination has become a popular choice for developers building scalable, cost-efficient APIs.

This introduction will guide you through the fundamental concepts of serverless computing, why Flask is an ideal framework for serverless development, the key benefits of using serverless architectures, and what you can expect to learn throughout this book. Finally, we'll help you get started by setting up your development environment for building serverless APIs with Flask.

The Evolution of API Development

To fully appreciate the rise of serverless computing, it's essential to understand the evolution of API development and how technological advancements have shifted the way we build and deploy applications.

1. **Traditional Monolithic Architectures** In the early days of web

development, applications were often built using monolithic architectures, where all components of an application were tightly coupled into a single unit. This included the user interface, business logic, and data layers. APIs, if present, were bundled into this monolithic structure. These applications ran on dedicated servers, which had to be provisioned, maintained, and scaled manually by developers or system administrators.
2. Monolithic architectures presented several challenges:

- **Scaling Issues**: As traffic grew, scaling a monolithic application required duplicating the entire system, leading to inefficiencies and higher costs.
- **Maintenance**: Any updates or changes required redeploying the entire system, increasing the risk of downtime.
- **Resource Management**: Server provisioning and resource management were complex and required significant expertise.

1. **The Rise of Microservices** As applications became more complex and the need for flexibility grew, developers started breaking down monolithic applications into smaller, independent components, known as microservices. Each microservice could be developed, deployed, and scaled independently. APIs played a crucial role in microservices architectures, allowing these independent services to communicate with each other and with front-end applications.
2. Microservices brought several benefits:

- **Improved Scalability**: Each service could be scaled independently based on demand.
- **Faster Development Cycles**: Teams could work on different services simultaneously, reducing the time to deploy new features.
- **Resilience**: If one service failed, the rest of the application could continue to function, improving overall system reliability.

INTRODUCTION

1. However, microservices also introduced new challenges, particularly in terms of managing the infrastructure required to support them. As the number of services grew, so did the need for more servers and resources, leading to increased complexity in managing deployments, scaling, and monitoring.
2. **Cloud Computing and Containerization** With the advent of cloud computing, developers gained access to on-demand, scalable computing resources. Cloud platforms like Amazon Web Services (AWS), Google Cloud Platform (GCP), and Microsoft Azure enabled developers to rent servers, storage, and other infrastructure as needed. This shift reduced the need for physical servers and made it easier to deploy and scale applications.
3. Containerization, led by technologies like Docker and Kubernetes, further revolutionized API development. Containers allowed developers to package applications and their dependencies into lightweight, portable units that could run consistently across different environments. Containers simplified deployment and scaling, but still required developers to manage the underlying infrastructure, including virtual machines, networking, and storage.
4. **The Serverless Revolution** Serverless computing, also known as Function-as-a-Service (FaaS), represents the next stage in the evolution of API development. In a serverless architecture, developers no longer need to manage servers or containers. Instead, they write functions or small units of code that are triggered by events, and the cloud provider automatically provisions, scales, and manages the necessary infrastructure.
5. The most popular serverless platform is AWS Lambda, which allows developers to run code in response to events without provisioning or managing servers. Other platforms like Google Cloud Functions and Azure Functions provide similar capabilities.
6. Serverless architectures offer several advantages over traditional and microservices architectures:

3

- **No Server Management**: Developers only focus on writing code, and the cloud provider takes care of provisioning, scaling, and maintaining servers.
- **Automatic Scaling**: Serverless platforms automatically scale functions in response to demand, ensuring that applications can handle sudden spikes in traffic without manual intervention.
- **Cost-Efficiency**: In a serverless model, developers are charged based on actual usage (e.g., the number of function executions), rather than paying for idle server time.
- **Faster Time to Market**: With serverless, developers can focus on building features rather than managing infrastructure, leading to faster development cycles.

1. APIs built using serverless architectures are highly scalable, cost-efficient, and flexible, making them ideal for modern applications.

Why Choose Flask for Serverless APIs?

Flask has gained widespread popularity as a lightweight and flexible micro-framework for building web applications and APIs in Python. It is an excellent choice for developers looking to build serverless APIs for several reasons:

1. **Minimalistic and Flexible** Flask is a "micro" framework, meaning it provides the basic tools needed to build web applications without imposing too many decisions on the developer. Unlike full-stack frameworks like Django, Flask allows developers to choose their own libraries, tools, and extensions, making it highly flexible. This flexibility is especially valuable in a serverless context, where developers often need to optimize code for specific functions or services.
2. **Python's Popularity and Ecosystem** Python is one of the most popular programming languages, particularly in the fields of web development, data science, and machine learning. Flask benefits from Python's vast ecosystem of libraries, tools, and community support.

This makes it easier for developers to integrate Flask APIs with other Python-based tools and services, such as machine learning models or data processing pipelines, in a serverless environment.

3. **Simple and Easy to Learn** Flask's simplicity makes it an ideal choice for developers of all experience levels. Its learning curve is gentle compared to more complex frameworks, meaning developers can get up and running with serverless Flask APIs quickly. Flask's clear and concise documentation further aids in this ease of use, making it accessible to beginners and experts alike.

4. **Compatibility with Serverless Frameworks** Flask integrates well with serverless frameworks such as AWS Lambda (via Zappa), Google Cloud Functions, and Azure Functions. Tools like Zappa make it easy to deploy Flask applications to a serverless environment, handling tasks like API Gateway setup, scaling, and monitoring. This compatibility simplifies the process of taking an existing Flask application and converting it to a fully serverless architecture.

5. **Efficient for API Development** Flask was designed with simplicity in mind, and its routing system is particularly well-suited for building APIs. Flask makes it easy to define RESTful endpoints, handle HTTP requests, and return JSON responses—essential components of an API. With extensions like Flask-RESTful, developers can build APIs more efficiently, adding features like request parsing, input validation, and response formatting.

6. **Modular Design** Flask's modular design allows developers to add only the components they need. This is important in serverless environments, where minimizing the size of your code package can reduce cold start times (the delay experienced when a serverless function is invoked for the first time or after a period of inactivity). Flask's modularity ensures that you only include the necessary libraries and extensions, improving performance in serverless deployments.

Benefits of Serverless Architectures: Scalability, Cost-Effectiveness, and Flexibility

The primary appeal of serverless architectures is the ability to build scalable, cost-efficient, and flexible applications without worrying about the underlying infrastructure. Below are some of the key benefits that serverless architectures offer, particularly when building APIs with Flask:

1. **Scalability** One of the most significant challenges in traditional API development is scaling applications to handle increasing traffic. In a serverless architecture, scaling is handled automatically by the cloud provider. As the number of API requests increases, the serverless platform spins up additional instances of the function to handle the load. This horizontal scaling happens seamlessly, without any need for manual intervention.

- **Automatic Scaling**: Serverless platforms like AWS Lambda automatically scale based on the number of requests, meaning your Flask API can handle sudden spikes in traffic without requiring additional infrastructure.
- **Granular Resource Allocation**: Instead of provisioning entire servers, serverless platforms allocate resources (memory and CPU) per request, ensuring that you're only charged for what you use.

1. **Cost-Effectiveness** Traditional server-based architectures require you to provision servers that run 24/7, even during periods of low traffic. With serverless, you're only billed for the actual execution time of your functions. This usage-based pricing model makes serverless architectures highly cost-efficient, especially for applications with variable traffic patterns.

- **Pay-Per-Use Model**: In serverless architectures, you are charged based on the number of function executions and the time it takes to execute them, rather than paying for idle server time.
- **No Upfront Costs**: There are no upfront costs for serverless services; you only pay for the resources consumed during function execution,

reducing overall operational costs.

1. **Flexibility** Serverless architectures provide developers with the flexibility to focus on writing code without worrying about server provisioning, scaling, or maintenance. Additionally, serverless platforms offer integrations with a wide range of cloud services, enabling developers to build complex applications with minimal effort.

- **Event-Driven Architecture**: Serverless functions can be triggered by various events, such as HTTP requests, database changes, or file uploads, making it easy to build event-driven APIs.
- **Multi-Cloud and Hybrid Solutions**: Serverless platforms are available across multiple cloud providers, allowing developers to build solutions that work across different environments.

What You'll Learn in This Book

This book is designed to provide a comprehensive guide to building serverless APIs with Flask. Whether you're a beginner looking to get started with Flask or an experienced developer interested in learning about serverless architecture, this book will provide valuable insights and practical examples. Here's a preview of what you'll learn:

1. **Introduction to Flask and Serverless Architectures**: You'll start by learning the basics of Flask and the core principles of serverless computing. This will include setting up your first Flask application and deploying it to a serverless platform like AWS Lambda.
2. **Building and Deploying Flask APIs**: You'll learn how to create RESTful APIs using Flask and deploy them to the cloud using serverless frameworks like Zappa and AWS Lambda. You'll also explore other serverless platforms such as Google Cloud Functions and Azure Functions.
3. **Scaling and Securing Flask APIs**: You'll discover how to handle scaling for Flask APIs in a serverless environment and implement

security best practices, including authentication, authorization, and data protection.
4. **Database Integration and Serverless Functions**: You'll explore how to integrate Flask APIs with serverless databases like AWS DynamoDB and how to manage serverless functions efficiently.
5. **CI/CD for Serverless Flask APIs**: You'll learn how to implement continuous integration and deployment (CI/CD) pipelines for your serverless Flask APIs, automating the process of deploying, testing, and monitoring your APIs in the cloud.
6. **Cost Optimization and Future Trends**: Finally, you'll discover strategies for optimizing costs in a serverless architecture and explore future trends in serverless API development, such as edge computing and AI integration.

Setting Up Your Development Environment

Before we dive into building serverless APIs with Flask, it's important to set up your development environment properly. Here's what you'll need:

1. **Python Installation**: Flask is a Python-based framework, so you'll need Python installed on your machine. You can download the latest version of Python from the official website.
2. **Flask Installation**: Once Python is installed, you can install Flask using pip, the Python package manager. Run the following command in your terminal or command prompt:

```bash
Copy code
pip install Flask
```

1. **AWS CLI Installation**: Since we'll be deploying Flask applications to AWS Lambda, you'll need to install the AWS Command Line Interface

(CLI). You can download it from the AWS CLI official documentation.
2. **Serverless Framework Installation**: If you plan to use the Serverless Framework to deploy Flask applications, install it globally on your machine using npm:

```bash
Copy code
npm install -g serverless
```

1. **Zappa Installation**: Zappa is a popular tool for deploying Python-based applications (like Flask) to AWS Lambda. Install Zappa using pip:

```bash
Copy code
pip install zappa
```

1. **AWS Account**: You'll need an AWS account to deploy your Flask APIs to AWS Lambda. If you don't already have one, you can create a free account on the AWS website.
2. **Text Editor or IDE**: Finally, choose a text editor or Integrated Development Environment (IDE) for writing your Flask code. Popular choices include Visual Studio Code, PyCharm, or Sublime Text.

Chapter 1: Getting Started with Flask and Serverless Architecture

Serverless architecture represents a paradigm shift in the way modern applications, particularly APIs, are developed and deployed. In this chapter, we will delve into the basics of Flask, a lightweight web framework that perfectly complements serverless development. We will also explore the principles of serverless computing, compare Flask with other web frameworks, guide you through the creation of your first Flask application, and introduce you to AWS Lambda and other serverless platforms.

Introduction to Flask

Flask is a Python micro-framework designed for building web applications quickly and with minimal setup. It's highly flexible, allowing developers to choose their own tools, libraries, and architecture. Flask doesn't require you to use specific tools or libraries, but it provides everything you need to build robust web applications and APIs.

The Philosophy Behind Flask

Flask follows the principle of **minimalism**. It is intentionally simple, yet it provides powerful tools for extending its capabilities as your application grows. This makes Flask an ideal choice for small projects as well as larger applications that require scalability. Some of the key principles of Flask are:

- **Minimalistic**: Flask doesn't come with too many pre-built components, giving developers the freedom to integrate libraries and tools of their choice.
- **Flexible**: Flask allows you to decide how you want to structure your application, letting you build everything from small APIs to large-scale applications.
- **Extensible**: Flask can easily be extended with a wide range of third-party libraries and plugins, such as Flask-SQLAlchemy for database integration or Flask-RESTful for building REST APIs.

Why Flask?

Flask is often chosen for its balance of simplicity and power. Unlike other more opinionated frameworks like Django, Flask allows you to start small and scale up as your project grows. This flexibility is particularly useful in serverless environments, where the lightweight nature of Flask helps reduce cold start times and ensures efficient use of resources.

Some specific reasons why Flask is an excellent choice for serverless architecture include:

1. **Lightweight**: The minimal footprint of Flask means less overhead and faster load times, which is crucial in a serverless environment.
2. **Modular**: Flask allows you to include only the libraries and extensions you need, making it highly customizable for different projects.
3. **Community Support**: Flask has a strong community and a vast ecosystem of libraries and extensions, providing extensive resources and tools for developers.
4. **Python-Based**: Python is widely used in data science, machine learning, and cloud computing, making Flask a natural fit for projects that need to integrate with these domains.

Key Components of Flask

Flask provides several key components that are useful for building APIs and web applications:

- **Routing**: Flask allows you to define routes (URLs) and map them to Python functions. This is essential for building APIs that respond to HTTP requests.
- **Request and Response Handling**: Flask makes it easy to handle incoming requests (GET, POST, etc.) and send appropriate responses, including JSON data.
- **Jinja2 Templating**: Flask includes support for Jinja2, a powerful templating engine that allows you to dynamically generate HTML, making it ideal for building web front-ends.
- **Middleware**: Flask supports middleware, which lets you process requests and responses before they reach your application or after they leave it. This is useful for tasks like logging, security, and input validation.
- **Extensions**: Flask has a rich ecosystem of extensions that add functionality such as database integration, authentication, and more. Popular extensions include Flask-RESTful (for building REST APIs), Flask-SQLAlchemy (for database integration), and Flask-Login (for user authentication).

Basics of Serverless Computing

Serverless computing is a cloud-computing execution model in which the cloud provider dynamically manages the allocation and provisioning of servers. With serverless, developers no longer need to worry about the infrastructure or servers. Instead, they can focus solely on writing code, and the cloud provider takes care of everything else, from scaling to maintenance.

How Does Serverless Work?

In a serverless architecture, you write small, stateless functions that are triggered by events. These functions are deployed to a cloud provider, such as AWS, Google Cloud, or Azure, which handles the following:

1. **Provisioning**: The cloud provider automatically provisions the necessary infrastructure to run your functions.
2. **Scaling**: Serverless functions automatically scale based on the number

of incoming requests, without any manual intervention.
3. **Billing**: You only pay for the actual execution time of your functions, rather than for maintaining idle servers.

Common serverless platforms include AWS Lambda, Google Cloud Functions, and Azure Functions. These platforms provide the infrastructure to run your code and automatically handle scaling, monitoring, and security.

Key Concepts in Serverless Architecture

- **Functions as a Service (FaaS)**: Serverless computing is often referred to as Functions as a Service (FaaS). In this model, individual functions are written and deployed to the cloud, where they are executed in response to events such as HTTP requests or changes to a database.
- **Event-Driven**: Serverless functions are triggered by events. These events can include API requests, file uploads, database changes, or scheduled tasks.
- **Stateless**: Serverless functions are stateless, meaning they do not retain data between executions. Any necessary data must be passed into the function or retrieved from external storage.
- **Auto-Scaling**: Serverless platforms automatically scale based on demand. If your application experiences a surge in traffic, the cloud provider will automatically allocate more resources to handle the load.
- **Cold Starts**: One of the challenges of serverless computing is cold starts. When a serverless function is invoked after a period of inactivity, the cloud provider must "spin up" the necessary infrastructure, leading to a delay. Minimizing cold starts is an important consideration when designing serverless applications.

Advantages of Serverless Computing

- **No Server Management**: Developers don't need to worry about provisioning, managing, or maintaining servers. The cloud provider handles all infrastructure tasks.

- **Automatic Scaling**: Serverless platforms automatically scale your application in response to demand, ensuring that your API can handle traffic spikes without manual intervention.
- **Cost Efficiency**: You only pay for the resources your application uses. This is particularly beneficial for applications with unpredictable traffic patterns, as you are not charged for idle resources.
- **Rapid Development**: With serverless, you can focus entirely on writing code, leading to faster development cycles and shorter time-to-market for applications.

Challenges of Serverless Computing

- **Cold Starts**: As mentioned, serverless functions may experience cold starts, which can introduce latency when functions are invoked after a period of inactivity.
- **Statelessness**: Since serverless functions are stateless, developers need to manage state externally, which can add complexity to certain applications.
- **Vendor Lock-In**: Different cloud providers have their own serverless platforms and services, which can lead to vendor lock-in if you build your application heavily around one provider's offerings.
- **Limited Execution Time**: Serverless functions typically have execution time limits (e.g., 15 minutes on AWS Lambda), making them unsuitable for long-running tasks.

Flask vs. Other Web Frameworks for Serverless

While Flask is a popular choice for serverless development, it's not the only web framework available. In this section, we'll compare Flask with other popular frameworks, focusing on their suitability for serverless architectures.

Flask vs. Django

Django is a full-stack Python web framework that comes with many built-in features such as an ORM (Object-Relational Mapper), an admin interface, and user authentication. While Django is highly feature-rich, its heavyweight nature can make it less suitable for serverless architectures.

- **Lightweight vs. Heavyweight**: Flask is minimalistic and lightweight, whereas Django is a full-featured framework that includes many built-in components. Flask's lightweight nature makes it more suitable for serverless environments where minimizing cold start times and reducing resource usage is critical.
- **Flexibility**: Flask gives developers complete control over which libraries and tools to use, while Django enforces a more structured approach. In serverless environments, Flask's flexibility is often an advantage, as you can choose the tools that best fit your needs.
- **Performance**: Flask generally has better performance in serverless environments because of its smaller footprint. Django's additional components can slow down performance, especially when cold starts are an issue.
- **Use Case**: If you're building a serverless API or a microservice, Flask is a better choice due to its simplicity and lightweight nature. If you're building a larger application that requires many built-in features, Django might be more appropriate, though it may not be the best fit for serverless architectures.

Flask vs. FastAPI

FastAPI is a relatively new Python framework that focuses on performance and ease of use. It is built on Python's type hints and asynchronous programming, making it one of the fastest frameworks available for building APIs.

- **Performance**: FastAPI is faster than Flask, thanks to its asynchronous capabilities and reliance on Python's modern features like type hints. If performance is a critical factor in your serverless application, FastAPI may be worth considering.
- **Ease of Use**: Both Flask and FastAPI are relatively easy to use. However,

FastAPI's automatic generation of API documentation (using OpenAPI and Swagger) makes it particularly developer-friendly.
- **Asynchronous Support**: FastAPI has built-in support for asynchronous programming, which can lead to better performance in serverless architectures where non-blocking I/O operations are common. Flask, on the other hand, requires additional extensions to support asynchronous programming.

Flask vs. Node.js (Express)

Express is a minimalistic web framework for Node.js and is commonly used for building APIs. It's often compared to Flask because both frameworks are lightweight and flexible.

- **Language**: Flask is built on Python, while Express is built on JavaScript (Node.js). The choice between Flask and Express often comes down to language preference. Both frameworks are suitable for serverless architectures.
- **Performance**: Node.js is known for its non-blocking I/O model, which can lead to better performance in certain types of serverless applications. However, Flask's performance is also excellent for many API use cases, and Python's simplicity makes it a popular choice for serverless development.
- **Ecosystem**: Flask benefits from Python's rich ecosystem of libraries and tools, particularly in areas like data science and machine learning. Express benefits from the vast JavaScript ecosystem, which is particularly strong in front-end development and real-time applications.

Creating Your First Flask Application

Now that you have a basic understanding of Flask and serverless computing, let's walk through the process of creating your first Flask application. This will serve as the foundation for building serverless APIs throughout the book.

Step 1: Setting Up Your Environment

CHAPTER 1: GETTING STARTED WITH FLASK AND SERVERLESS...

Before you start coding, make sure you have the necessary tools installed on your machine:

1. **Python**: Ensure you have Python installed. You can check your Python version by running python —version in your terminal or command prompt.
2. **Flask**: Install Flask using pip:

```bash
Copy code
pip install Flask
```

Step 2: Creating a Basic Flask Application

Once Flask is installed, you can create a simple Flask application. Here's a basic example:

```python
Copy code
from flask import Flask

app = Flask(__name__)

@app.route('/')
def hello_world():
    return 'Hello, World!'

if __name__ == '__main__':
    app.run(debug=True)
```

Let's break down the code:

- **Flask Object**: The Flask class creates a Flask application. __name__ is passed to the Flask constructor to indicate the location of the application.
- **Route**: The @app.route('/') decorator defines a route for the root URL

(/). When a user navigates to this URL, the hello_world function is executed, and the string 'Hello, World!' is returned as the response.
- **Running the Application**: The if __name__ == '__main__' block ensures that the application runs only if the script is executed directly. The app.run(debug=True) line starts the Flask development server with debugging enabled.

To run the application, save the file as app.py and run the following command in your terminal:

```bash
Copy code
python app.py
```

Navigate to http://127.0.0.1:5000/ in your browser, and you should see the message "Hello, World!" This is your first Flask application in action!

Step 3: Adding Routes and Functionality

You can easily add more routes to your Flask application. For example, let's add a new route that returns JSON data:

```python
Copy code
@app.route('/api/data')
def get_data():
    return {'name': 'Flask API', 'version': '1.0'}
```

This route returns a simple JSON object. Flask makes it easy to create APIs by returning Python dictionaries, which are automatically converted to JSON responses.

You can test the new route by navigating to http://127.0.0.1:5000/api/data in your browser or using a tool like Postman or curl.

Introduction to AWS Lambda and Other Serverless Platforms

Now that you've created a basic Flask application, let's explore how to deploy it to a serverless platform, starting with AWS Lambda. AWS Lambda is one of the most popular serverless platforms and is commonly used for deploying serverless APIs.

What is AWS Lambda?

AWS Lambda is a serverless computing service provided by Amazon Web Services. It allows you to run code in response to events without provisioning or managing servers. Lambda automatically scales your application based on the number of incoming requests, and you only pay for the actual execution time of your functions.

Some key features of AWS Lambda include:

- **Event-Driven**: Lambda functions are triggered by events, such as HTTP requests, changes to an S3 bucket, or database updates.
- **Auto-Scaling**: Lambda automatically scales your functions in response to demand, so you don't need to worry about provisioning servers.
- **Cost-Effective**: With Lambda, you only pay for the time your code is executed, making it highly cost-efficient for applications with variable traffic patterns.

Other Serverless Platforms

While AWS Lambda is the most well-known serverless platform, other cloud providers offer similar services:

1. **Google Cloud Functions**: Google's serverless platform allows you to run code in response to events on Google Cloud.
2. **Azure Functions**: Microsoft's Azure Functions is a serverless platform that supports a wide range of triggers, including HTTP requests, timers, and database changes.
3. **IBM Cloud Functions**: IBM offers serverless computing with support for multiple programming languages and integrations with IBM's cloud services.

Each platform has its own strengths, and the choice of platform often depends on your specific requirements and the cloud services you are already using.

Deploying Flask to AWS Lambda Using Zappa

Zappa is a popular tool for deploying Python-based applications, such as Flask, to AWS Lambda. Zappa handles the deployment process, including setting up API Gateway, configuring Lambda functions, and managing scaling.

To deploy your Flask application to AWS Lambda using Zappa, follow these steps:

1. **Install Zappa**:

```bash
Copy code
pip install zappa
```

1. **Initialize Zappa**: In your Flask project directory, run the following command to initialize Zappa:

```bash
Copy code
zappa init
```

1. Follow the prompts to configure your Zappa deployment. Zappa will automatically set up the necessary AWS resources, including API Gateway and Lambda.
2. **Deploy Your Application**:

```bash
Copy code
zappa deploy
```

1. Zappa will deploy your Flask application to AWS Lambda and provide you with an API Gateway URL. You can use this URL to access your Flask API.

Once deployed, your Flask application is fully serverless, automatically scaling based on traffic and benefiting from the cost-efficiency of AWS Lambda.

Chapter 2: Building and Deploying Your First Serverless Flask API

Serverless development has revolutionized how developers create, deploy, and maintain applications. With the combination of Flask and serverless architecture, developers can build scalable, cost-effective APIs without worrying about the complexity of infrastructure management. In this chapter, we will cover the essential steps to build and deploy your first serverless Flask API. You will gain an understanding of the serverless workflow, how to set up Flask for serverless deployments, how to deploy your API to AWS Lambda using Zappa, how to test your API endpoints, and how to troubleshoot common issues that may arise during the deployment process.

Understanding the Serverless Workflow

The serverless workflow differs significantly from traditional server-based application deployment. In server-based applications, you need to provision and maintain servers, configure load balancers, and ensure that your application scales as traffic increases. However, in a serverless architecture, much of this work is handled by the cloud provider.

The serverless model allows you to focus solely on writing code. You don't need to worry about managing servers or scaling infrastructure. Instead, your code runs as small, stateless functions that respond to specific events, such as an HTTP request, a database update, or a file upload. When an event occurs, the serverless platform automatically provisions the required resources, runs the function, and returns the result.

Here's a basic workflow for serverless application development:
1. **Write Code**: As the developer, you focus on writing functions or API endpoints. These functions are small, stateless pieces of code that respond to events.
2. **Deploy to Serverless Platform**: You deploy your code to a serverless platform such as AWS Lambda, Google Cloud Functions, or Azure Functions. The platform handles all server provisioning, scaling, and resource allocation.
3. **Event Triggers**: Events such as HTTP requests, database changes, or scheduled tasks trigger your functions. For API development, events are usually HTTP requests sent to API endpoints.
4. **Execution**: When the event occurs, the serverless platform spins up a container, executes your code, and returns the result. This process happens automatically, and you are charged only for the time your function is running.
5. **Auto-Scaling**: If multiple events occur simultaneously (e.g., multiple API requests), the serverless platform scales automatically by running multiple instances of your function in parallel. This ensures your application can handle traffic spikes without manual intervention.
6. **Monitoring and Maintenance**: The cloud provider manages infrastructure-level monitoring, scaling, and maintenance. You can focus on monitoring performance metrics and optimizing your application code rather than worrying about infrastructure.

Serverless Workflow for Flask API Development

When you use Flask in a serverless environment, your Flask application runs as a series of serverless functions. Instead of running your Flask app on a traditional server, you deploy it as a set of functions that respond to HTTP requests via an API Gateway, which routes the requests to the appropriate function in AWS Lambda or another serverless platform.

For example, when a user makes a request to a Flask API endpoint, an API Gateway routes the request to the corresponding Lambda function. The function processes the request, interacts with any necessary databases or services, and returns a response, typically in JSON format.

Here's a high-level view of how Flask fits into the serverless workflow:

- **Routing HTTP Requests**: Flask routes incoming HTTP requests to the appropriate functions.
- **API Gateway**: In a serverless architecture, an API Gateway acts as a "front door" for HTTP requests. It passes requests to Lambda functions, which execute Flask code.
- **AWS Lambda**: Flask functions are deployed to AWS Lambda, where they are executed in response to events (e.g., HTTP requests).
- **Scaling**: AWS Lambda automatically scales the Flask API in response to traffic, running multiple instances of your functions as needed.

Setting Up Flask for Serverless Deployments

To deploy Flask applications in a serverless environment, you need to make some adjustments to your setup. We'll focus on AWS Lambda as the serverless platform and Zappa as the deployment tool in this chapter.

1. Install Zappa

Zappa is a popular tool for deploying Python-based applications, such as Flask, to AWS Lambda. Zappa automates the process of packaging, deploying, and managing Flask applications on AWS Lambda. It simplifies the deployment process and handles tasks such as setting up API Gateway, scaling, and monitoring.

To install Zappa, use the following pip command:

```bash
Copy code
pip install zappa
```

This installs Zappa globally on your system, allowing you to use it for deploying Flask applications.

2. Configure AWS Credentials

Before deploying your Flask API to AWS Lambda, you need to configure your AWS credentials. This will allow Zappa to communicate with your AWS account and deploy the necessary resources.

If you don't already have the AWS Command Line Interface (CLI) installed, you can install it by following the instructions on the AWS CLI Installation Guide.

Once the AWS CLI is installed, you can configure your AWS credentials by running:

```bash
Copy code
aws configure
```

You will be prompted to enter your AWS Access Key ID, AWS Secret Access Key, region, and output format. These credentials allow Zappa to deploy your Flask application to AWS Lambda.

3. Initialize Zappa in Your Flask Project

After installing Zappa and configuring your AWS credentials, navigate to the root directory of your Flask project and initialize Zappa using the following command:

```bash
Copy code
zappa init
```

Zappa will guide you through a series of prompts to set up your deployment configuration. You'll be asked for details such as the name of your project, the desired AWS region, and whether you want to deploy to an existing or new S3 bucket.

Zappa will generate a zappa_settings.json file in your project directory, which contains the configuration settings for your serverless deployment.

Here's an example of a basic zappa_settings.json file:

```json
Copy code
{
    "dev": {
        "app_function": "app.app",
        "aws_region": "us-east-1",
        "s3_bucket": "your-bucket-name",
        "timeout_seconds": 30,
        "memory_size": 128,
        "keep_warm": true
    }
}
```

- **app_function**: This specifies the Python path to your Flask application. In this case, it points to the app object in the app.py file.
- **aws_region**: The AWS region where your Lambda function will be deployed.
- **s3_bucket**: Zappa uses an S3 bucket to store deployment packages. You can specify an existing bucket or create a new one during the zappa init process.
- **timeout_seconds**: This specifies how long AWS Lambda will wait for a function to complete before timing out.
- **memory_size**: This sets the amount of memory allocated to the Lambda function. Adjust this value based on your application's requirements.
- **keep_warm**: This setting keeps your Lambda function "warm" by periodically invoking it, reducing cold start times.

4. Modifying Flask Application for Serverless

Flask applications are generally designed to run on a web server, but when deploying to AWS Lambda, you need to make sure that your application is compatible with the serverless environment.

You should design your Flask routes as small, self-contained functions that are stateless. AWS Lambda functions are stateless by nature, meaning that any data or state needed for processing must be passed into the function or stored externally in a database or service.

Here's a simple Flask API that we'll use for deployment:

```python
Copy code
from flask import Flask, jsonify

app = Flask(__name__)

@app.route('/')
def home():
    return jsonify({"message": "Welcome to your first serverless
    Flask API!"})

@app.route('/api/data')
def get_data():
    return jsonify({"data": "This is some serverless data!"})

if __name__ == '__main__':
    app.run(debug=True)
```

This Flask application contains two routes: the root (/) and an API route (/api/data). Both return JSON responses, which is typical for APIs.

Now that your Flask application is set up, it's ready to be deployed to AWS Lambda using Zappa.

Deploying a Simple Flask API to AWS Lambda Using Zappa

With your Flask application and Zappa configured, it's time to deploy the API to AWS Lambda. Zappa makes this process easy with just a few simple commands.

1. Initial Deployment

To deploy your Flask API to AWS Lambda, run the following command:

```bash
Copy code
zappa deploy dev
```

This command tells Zappa to package your Flask application, upload it to AWS Lambda, and create the necessary API Gateway routes. The dev argument refers to the deployment environment, which corresponds to the settings in the zappa_settings.json file.

Zappa will output the progress of the deployment, including the creation of resources such as the Lambda function, API Gateway, and S3 bucket.

Once the deployment is complete, Zappa will provide you with an API Gateway URL, which you can use to access your serverless Flask API.

Example output:

```bash
Copy code
Deploying API Gateway..
Deployment complete!
Your API is live at:
https://1234567890.execute-api.us-east-1.amazonaws.com/dev
```

You can visit the provided URL in your browser or use tools like Postman or curl to interact with your serverless Flask API.

2. Updating the API

As you develop your Flask API further, you'll likely need to make updates to your code. To deploy these updates to AWS Lambda, use the zappa update command:

```bash
Copy code
zappa update dev
```

This
 will package the updated Flask application and deploy the changes to AWS

Lambda.

3. Managing Your API

Zappa provides several commands for managing your serverless Flask API:

- **zappa status dev**: Check the status of your deployment, including information about your Lambda function and API Gateway.
- **zappa tail dev**: View the real-time logs from your Lambda function.
- **zappa rollback dev**: Roll back your deployment to a previous version.
- **zappa undeploy dev**: Remove your Flask API from AWS Lambda and delete associated resources such as API Gateway.

Testing Your API Endpoints in a Serverless Environment

After deploying your Flask API to AWS Lambda, it's essential to test the API endpoints to ensure they are working correctly and returning the expected results. Testing serverless APIs is similar to testing traditional APIs, but there are a few additional considerations related to serverless environments, such as cold starts and scaling behavior.

1. Testing with a Web Browser

For simple tests, you can use a web browser to access your API's endpoints. For example, if your API Gateway URL is https://1234567890.execute-api.us-east-1.amazonaws.com/dev, you can visit the following URLs in your browser:

- **Home Route**: https://1234567890.execute-api.us-east-1.amazonaws.com/dev/
- **API Data Route**: https://1234567890.execute-api.us-east-1.amazonaws.com/dev/api/data

If your API is functioning correctly, you should see the JSON responses defined in your Flask routes.

2. Testing with Postman

Postman is a popular tool for testing APIs. It allows you to send requests to your API and view the responses, making it easier to test various HTTP methods (GET, POST, PUT, DELETE) and headers.

To test your serverless Flask API using Postman:

1. Open Postman and create a new request.
2. Set the request method to GET.
3. Enter the API Gateway URL followed by the route you want to test (e.g., /api/data).
4. Click "Send" and check the response.

You should receive a JSON response from the server.

3. Testing with curl

If you prefer to use the command line, curl is a handy tool for testing API endpoints. Here's how you can test the /api/data route with curl:

```bash
Copy code
curl https://1234567890.execute-api.us-east-1.amazonaws.com/dev/api/data
```

This command sends a GET request to your API and outputs the JSON response.

4. Monitoring API Performance

AWS provides several tools for monitoring the performance of your serverless API:

- **Amazon CloudWatch**: AWS Lambda integrates with CloudWatch, which allows you to view metrics such as invocation counts, execution duration, and errors. CloudWatch is useful for monitoring the performance of your API and identifying potential issues, such as slow response times or failed requests.
- **API Gateway Logs**: You can enable detailed logging for API Gateway, which provides insights into the requests and responses processed by your API. This can help you troubleshoot issues related to request

routing or input validation.

Common Pitfalls and Troubleshooting

While deploying and managing serverless APIs is generally straightforward, there are some common issues that developers may encounter. Here are some potential pitfalls and tips for troubleshooting your Flask API in a serverless environment.

1. Cold Starts

A cold start occurs when a Lambda function is invoked for the first time or after a period of inactivity. The serverless platform needs to spin up a container to run your function, which can introduce latency.

- **Solution**: Use Zappa's keep_warm setting to periodically invoke your Lambda function, keeping it "warm" and reducing the likelihood of cold starts. This setting is particularly useful for APIs that need to respond quickly to requests.

2. Timeout Issues

AWS Lambda has a default execution timeout of 3 seconds. If your function takes longer than the configured timeout to complete, AWS will terminate the function, and the request will fail.

- **Solution**: Increase the timeout setting in your zappa_settings.json file. For example, if your function takes up to 30 seconds to execute, set "timeout_seconds": 30 in your configuration.

3. Memory Limits

By default, Lambda functions are allocated 128 MB of memory. If your Flask API requires more memory to process requests (e.g., when handling large data sets), you may encounter out-of-memory errors.

- **Solution**: Increase the memory allocated to your Lambda function by modifying the "memory_size" setting in your zappa_settings.json file.

For example, "memory_size": 256 allocates 256 MB of memory to the function.

4. API Gateway Caching

If you notice slow response times for certain API routes, API Gateway caching may help improve performance by storing responses for frequently requested data.

- **Solution**: Enable caching for specific routes in API Gateway, which can reduce the load on your Lambda function and improve response times for common requests.

5. Debugging and Logs

When a Lambda function fails, the error is logged in Amazon CloudWatch. Reviewing these logs can help you identify the root cause of the issue.

- **Solution**: Use zappa tail dev to view real-time logs from your Lambda function. You can also configure additional logging in your Flask application to capture more detailed information about requests and responses.

With this chapter, you've taken your first step into the world of serverless Flask API development. You've learned how to build a simple Flask API, configure it for serverless deployment, and deploy it to AWS Lambda using Zappa. You've also explored techniques for testing and troubleshooting your serverless API.

Chapter 3: Scaling Flask APIs with AWS Lambda

Scalability is one of the most critical factors to consider when developing APIs. In traditional web application architectures, scaling involves manually configuring and maintaining servers to handle varying levels of traffic. However, serverless architecture, and specifically AWS Lambda, removes much of this burden by automatically scaling your applications in response to incoming traffic. This chapter will explore how Flask APIs scale with AWS Lambda, the auto-scaling features provided by Lambda, how to handle increased API traffic, monitoring API performance using AWS CloudWatch, and best practices for scaling Flask APIs in a serverless environment.

Understanding Serverless Scaling

Scaling in the context of web applications refers to the ability of the application to handle an increase in workload, whether it's due to increased users, larger data sets, or more frequent requests. Traditionally, scaling can be horizontal (adding more servers) or vertical (adding more resources to a single server). While both methods work, they require manual intervention, configuration, and often lead to over-provisioning of resources during low-traffic periods.

In serverless computing, scaling is handled automatically by the cloud provider. Instead of manually adding more servers or resources, the serverless platform dynamically adjusts based on demand, provisioning only what is necessary at any given time. This is particularly advantageous for API developers, as it ensures that your APIs can handle fluctuating levels of traffic without manual configuration.

Key characteristics of serverless scaling include:

- **Event-Driven Scaling**: Serverless functions scale in response to events, such as HTTP requests or database triggers. When an event occurs, the serverless platform provisions the necessary resources to handle the request.
- **Granular Resource Allocation**: Serverless platforms allocate resources at the function level, allowing for more efficient scaling compared to traditional server-based architectures, where entire servers must be scaled.
- **Auto-Scaling**: The serverless platform automatically adds or removes resources in response to traffic patterns, ensuring that your application can handle sudden spikes in traffic without downtime or performance degradation.

In the case of AWS Lambda, scaling occurs automatically at the function level. When a Flask API deployed to Lambda receives multiple requests, Lambda creates multiple instances of the function (also known as containers) to handle the requests. Each instance can handle one request at a time, and Lambda automatically manages the scaling process in response to the load.

Auto-Scaling Features of AWS Lambda

AWS Lambda is designed to scale automatically, providing a seamless experience for developers. The platform scales by running multiple concurrent instances of your function, each isolated from the others, so they can handle individual requests simultaneously. This automatic scaling is one of the core features of Lambda and a significant advantage for serverless API development.

Concurrency in AWS Lambda

Concurrency refers to the number of requests that AWS Lambda can handle simultaneously. Lambda handles concurrency by invoking new instances of your function when multiple requests come in at the same time. Each instance is stateless, meaning it does not retain any data between invocations.

- **Initial Concurrency**: When a Flask API receives its first request, AWS Lambda spins up an instance (container) to handle that request. This is known as a **cold start**, where the environment is initialized and prepared to run your function.
- **Subsequent Concurrency**: For subsequent requests, Lambda either reuses the existing instance if it is available or creates new instances to handle additional requests. The platform automatically manages the creation and termination of these instances, with no manual intervention required.
- **Provisioned Concurrency**: While Lambda handles scaling automatically, AWS also offers **Provisioned Concurrency** for applications that need to maintain a certain number of warm instances at all times. This reduces cold start latency, which can be critical for APIs with strict performance requirements.

AWS Lambda's default concurrency limit is 1,000 concurrent executions per region, but this limit can be increased by submitting a request to AWS. For most applications, the default concurrency limit is sufficient to handle typical traffic patterns.

Cold Starts and Warm Starts

One of the challenges of AWS Lambda's auto-scaling capabilities is managing **cold starts**. A cold start occurs when Lambda needs to spin up a new instance to handle a request, and this process introduces a small delay (usually between 100ms and 500ms). While cold starts are generally not an issue for occasional requests, they can become noticeable in high-traffic applications where low latency is critical.

- **Cold Start**: When a function is invoked after a period of inactivity,

Lambda needs to initialize the execution environment and load the function code. This process introduces a delay, which is known as a cold start.
- **Warm Start**: Once a Lambda function has been invoked, AWS keeps the function instance "warm" for a short period. If another request comes in while the instance is still warm, Lambda can reuse the instance, avoiding the cold start delay.

To mitigate the impact of cold starts, AWS Lambda provides the **Provisioned Concurrency** feature, which allows you to pre-allocate a set number of function instances to handle requests. These instances remain warm and ready to handle traffic, reducing latency.

Auto-Scaling Limits

While AWS Lambda's auto-scaling capabilities are powerful, there are some limits to consider:

- **Concurrency Limits**: As mentioned, the default concurrency limit is 1,000 concurrent executions per region. This limit can be increased by requesting a quota adjustment from AWS.
- **Burst Concurrency**: In addition to the default concurrency limit, Lambda allows for a burst of up to 500 additional concurrent executions in any region. This burst capacity can be useful for handling sudden spikes in traffic, but it is limited and may not be sufficient for extremely high-traffic applications.
- **Timeouts**: AWS Lambda functions have a maximum timeout of 15 minutes. If a request takes longer than this to process, Lambda will terminate the function. This limit is usually not an issue for typical Flask API requests, but it's important to design your APIs to handle requests efficiently and avoid long-running processes.

Handling Increased API Traffic with Flask

As your Flask API gains popularity, it's essential to ensure that it can handle increased traffic while maintaining performance and reliability. Serverless platforms like AWS Lambda make scaling easier, but there are still some best practices and considerations for optimizing your Flask application.

Optimizing Flask Code for Scalability

While AWS Lambda handles scaling at the infrastructure level, you still need to ensure that your Flask application is optimized to handle increased traffic. Here are some tips for optimizing Flask code for scalability:

1. **Stateless Design**: Ensure that your Flask routes are stateless. Serverless functions are inherently stateless, meaning they do not retain data between invocations. Any state that your application needs should be stored in external services, such as a database or a caching layer.
2. **Efficient Routing**: Flask's routing system is highly flexible, but it's important to keep your routes simple and efficient. Avoid complex route logic that could introduce unnecessary latency or complexity.
3. **Minimize Cold Starts**: While cold starts are primarily managed by AWS Lambda, there are some steps you can take to reduce their impact. For example, you can use Zappa's **keep_warm** setting to periodically invoke your Lambda function, keeping it warm and reducing cold start times.
4. **Use Caching**: Caching can significantly reduce the load on your Flask API by storing frequently accessed data in a cache, such as Redis or AWS ElastiCache. This reduces the need to repeatedly query a database or perform expensive computations.
5. **Avoid Long-Running Requests**: AWS Lambda has a maximum execution timeout of 15 minutes. To ensure that your Flask API does not exceed this limit, avoid long-running requests and break them into smaller, more manageable tasks if necessary. For example, if your API needs to process large amounts of data, consider breaking the task into smaller batches and using asynchronous processing.

Scaling Database Connections

As your Flask API scales, it's important to ensure that your database can also handle the increased traffic. Database bottlenecks are a common issue in high-traffic applications, especially when multiple concurrent requests are trying to access the same database resources.

Here are some strategies for scaling database connections in a serverless Flask API:

1. **Connection Pooling**: Use connection pooling to manage database connections efficiently. Connection pooling allows multiple requests to share a pool of database connections, reducing the overhead of establishing new connections for each request. For example, you can use an ORM like SQLAlchemy with connection pooling enabled.
2. **Read Replicas**: If your application performs a large number of read operations, consider using read replicas to distribute the load. AWS RDS allows you to create read replicas of your primary database, which can handle read-only traffic and reduce the load on your primary database instance.
3. **Optimize Queries**: Ensure that your database queries are optimized for performance. Avoid complex joins or expensive queries that could slow down your API. Use indexing and query optimization techniques to improve database performance.
4. **Serverless Databases**: Consider using a serverless database like AWS Aurora Serverless or DynamoDB, which automatically scales based on demand. Serverless databases can handle increased traffic without the need for manual scaling or configuration.

Handling API Rate Limits

As your Flask API scales, it's important to implement rate limiting to prevent abuse and ensure that your API can handle increased traffic without being overwhelmed. Rate limiting controls the number of requests that a user or client can make within a specified period, protecting your API from excessive traffic.

Here's how you can implement rate limiting in a serverless Flask API:

1. **Flask-Limiter Extension**: The Flask-Limiter extension provides an

easy way to implement rate limiting in Flask applications. You can set rate limits on specific routes or globally across your API.
2. **API Gateway Rate Limiting**: AWS API Gateway allows you to configure rate limiting at the gateway level, limiting the number of requests that can be sent to your Lambda functions. You can configure both burst limits (the maximum number of requests allowed in a short period) and steady-state limits (the average number of requests allowed over time).
3. **Custom Rate Limiting**: If you need more granular control over rate limiting, you can implement custom rate limiting logic using a caching layer like Redis. For example, you can store the number of requests made by each user in a Redis cache and reject requests that exceed the allowed limit.

By implementing rate limiting, you can protect your Flask API from being overwhelmed by excessive traffic and ensure that it remains responsive even under heavy load.

Monitoring Flask API Performance in AWS CloudWatch

Monitoring is a critical aspect of maintaining and scaling a serverless Flask API. AWS provides several tools for monitoring the performance of your Lambda functions, API Gateway, and other resources. CloudWatch is the primary monitoring service in AWS and provides a wealth of metrics and logs that can help you monitor and optimize your Flask API.

CloudWatch Metrics

CloudWatch provides real-time metrics for AWS Lambda and API Gateway, allowing you to monitor key performance indicators such as:

1. **Invocations**: The number of times your Lambda function has been invoked. This metric gives you insight into the overall traffic to your API.
2. **Duration**: The time it takes for your Lambda function to complete execution. Monitoring duration is essential for identifying performance bottlenecks and optimizing response times.

3. **Errors**: The number of errors encountered during Lambda function execution. Monitoring error rates can help you identify issues in your Flask API and take corrective action.
4. **Throttles**: The number of times your Lambda function has been throttled due to exceeding concurrency limits. If you see a high number of throttles, it may be time to request an increase in your concurrency limits or optimize your API to reduce resource usage.
5. **API Gateway Metrics**: CloudWatch also provides metrics for API Gateway, including the number of requests, latency, and error rates. These metrics are useful for monitoring the overall performance of your API and identifying issues such as slow response times or failed requests.

CloudWatch Logs

In addition to metrics, CloudWatch provides logs that capture detailed information about the execution of your Lambda functions. These logs can help you debug issues and gain insight into the behavior of your Flask API.

- **Log Streams**: CloudWatch creates a new log stream for each instance of your Lambda function. These log streams contain detailed information about the function execution, including any print statements or error messages.
- **Custom Logging**: You can add custom logging to your Flask API by using Python's logging module or the print() function. These logs will appear in CloudWatch and can be useful for debugging and monitoring specific parts of your application.
- **Log Retention**: By default, CloudWatch retains logs for an indefinite period. However, you can configure log retention policies to automatically delete old logs after a certain period, reducing storage costs.

Alarms and Notifications

CloudWatch allows you to create alarms based on specific metrics, such as the number of errors or the duration of Lambda function executions. You can configure these alarms to send notifications via Amazon SNS (Simple Notification Service) when thresholds are exceeded, allowing you to take immediate action to resolve issues.

For example, you can create an alarm that triggers when the error rate for your Lambda function exceeds a certain threshold. This alarm can send a notification to your team via email or SMS, allowing you to investigate and resolve the issue before it impacts your users.

Best Practices for Scaling Flask APIs in a Serverless World

Scaling Flask APIs in a serverless environment requires careful planning and optimization to ensure that your application can handle increased traffic without sacrificing performance or reliability. Here are some best practices for scaling Flask APIs with AWS Lambda:

1. Design for Statelessness

Serverless functions are inherently stateless, meaning they do not retain data between invocations. To scale effectively, ensure that your Flask API is designed to be stateless. Any data that needs to persist between requests should be stored in external services, such as a database or a caching layer.

2. Use Caching to Improve Performance

Caching can significantly reduce the load on your API and improve response times. Consider using a caching layer like Redis or AWS ElastiCache to store frequently accessed data, reducing the need to repeatedly query a database or perform expensive computations.

3. Implement Rate Limiting

Rate limiting protects your API from abuse and ensures that it can handle increased traffic without being overwhelmed. Use tools like Flask-Limiter or API Gateway's built-in rate limiting features to control the number of requests that each user or client can make.

4. Optimize Database Connections

As your API scales, it's important to ensure that your database can handle the increased traffic. Use connection pooling, read replicas, and query optimization techniques to improve database performance and reduce the likelihood of bottlenecks.

5. Monitor and Optimize Performance

Use CloudWatch to monitor the performance of your Flask API and identify potential issues such as slow response times, high error rates, or throttled requests. Set up alarms to notify you of performance issues, and take proactive steps to optimize your API for better scalability.

6. Minimize Cold Starts

Cold starts can introduce latency, especially in high-traffic applications. Use Zappa's keep_warm setting or AWS Lambda's **Provisioned Concurrency** feature to keep your Lambda functions warm and reduce the impact of cold starts.

7. Use Serverless Databases

Consider using serverless databases like AWS Aurora Serverless or DynamoDB, which automatically scale based on demand. Serverless databases can handle increased traffic without the need for manual configuration or scaling.

In this chapter, we explored how AWS Lambda handles scaling for Flask APIs, the auto-scaling features of AWS Lambda, and best practices for handling increased API traffic. You learned how to optimize Flask code for scalability, manage database connections, and implement rate limiting. We also covered monitoring API performance with AWS CloudWatch and provided best practices for scaling Flask APIs in a serverless environment.

Chapter 4: Securing Flask APIs in a Serverless Environment

In the realm of web development, security is a paramount concern, especially when it comes to APIs that serve as the backbone for many applications. As APIs become more prevalent in our interconnected world, securing them against unauthorized access, data breaches, and other malicious activities is crucial. This chapter delves into the security measures necessary for protecting Flask APIs deployed in a serverless environment, specifically focusing on AWS Lambda.

We'll explore the fundamental concepts of API security, delve into implementing authentication using OAuth2 and JSON Web Tokens (JWT), discuss the protective measures provided by API Gateway, cover rate limiting and throttling techniques, and examine how to secure data transmission with HTTPS and Cloudflare.

Introduction to API Security

API security encompasses the practices and technologies designed to protect APIs from various threats, including unauthorized access, data breaches, and abuse. With the rise of serverless architectures, where APIs are increasingly deployed in cloud environments, understanding and implementing robust security measures is more critical than ever.

Key Aspects of API Security

1. **Authentication**: Ensuring that users or applications are who they claim to be. Authentication is the first line of defense in API security, as it prevents unauthorized access to protected resources.
2. **Authorization**: Once a user is authenticated, authorization determines what resources or actions they are permitted to access. Effective authorization controls help mitigate risks related to privilege escalation.
3. **Data Integrity**: Ensuring that data sent over the network remains unchanged during transmission. Data integrity measures protect against man-in-the-middle attacks and tampering.
4. **Encryption**: Encrypting data in transit and at rest helps protect sensitive information from unauthorized access. Secure communication channels, such as HTTPS, are essential for API security.
5. **Input Validation**: Ensuring that incoming data meets certain criteria and does not contain malicious content. Proper input validation prevents attacks such as SQL injection and cross-site scripting (XSS).
6. **Rate Limiting**: Controlling the number of requests made to an API within a given timeframe helps protect against abuse, denial-of-service attacks, and unexpected spikes in traffic.
7. **Monitoring and Logging**: Continuously monitoring API usage and logging activities is essential for detecting suspicious behavior and investigating security incidents.

In serverless architectures, where APIs are often publicly accessible, applying these security principles is crucial. As we proceed, we will look closely at specific strategies for securing Flask APIs deployed in AWS Lambda.

Implementing Authentication with OAuth2 and JWT

Authentication is the process of verifying the identity of a user or application attempting to access your API. There are several methods for implementing authentication, but OAuth2 and JSON Web Tokens (JWT) are among the most widely used in modern API development.

Understanding OAuth2

OAuth2 is an authorization framework that enables applications to obtain limited access to user accounts on an HTTP service. It allows users to grant third-party applications access to their data without sharing their passwords. Instead of providing credentials, users authorize applications to act on their behalf using access tokens.

Key Components of OAuth2:

- **Resource Owner**: The user who owns the data and can grant access to it.
- **Client**: The application requesting access to the user's data.
- **Authorization Server**: The server responsible for authenticating the user and issuing access tokens.
- **Resource Server**: The server that hosts the protected resources (your API).

OAuth2 Workflow:

1. The user initiates an authentication request from the client application.
2. The client redirects the user to the authorization server, where the user logs in and grants permission.
3. The authorization server returns an authorization code to the client.
4. The client exchanges the authorization code for an access token.
5. The client uses the access token to access protected resources on the resource server (your API).

Using JWT for API Authentication

JSON Web Tokens (JWT) are a compact, URL-safe means of representing claims to be transferred between two parties. JWTs are widely used in API authentication due to their simplicity and ease of use.

Structure of a JWT: A JWT consists of three parts: Header, Payload, and Signature. They are base64-encoded and separated by periods.

1. **Header**: Contains metadata about the token, such as the algorithm used to sign the token (e.g., HMAC, SHA256).
2. **Payload**: Contains the claims or information about the user, such as

user ID, roles, and permissions.
3. **Signature**: A cryptographic signature generated using the header, payload, and a secret key. This signature ensures the integrity of the token.

JWT Authentication Workflow:

1. The user logs in with their credentials, and the server generates a JWT after validating the credentials.
2. The server sends the JWT back to the client, which stores it (typically in local storage).
3. For subsequent requests to protected API endpoints, the client includes the JWT in the Authorization header.
4. The server validates the JWT, checking its signature and expiration date before granting access to the requested resource.

Implementing OAuth2 and JWT in Flask: To implement OAuth2 and JWT in your Flask API, you can use libraries like Flask-OAuthlib for OAuth2 and PyJWT for JWT handling.

Example Code: Here's a simplified example of how to set up JWT authentication in a Flask API:

```python
Copy code
from flask import Flask, request, jsonify
import jwt
import datetime

app = Flask(__name__)
app.config['SECRET_KEY'] = 'your_secret_key'  # Change this to a secure key

# User data for demonstration purposes
users = {'user1': 'password1'}
```

```python
# Function to generate JWT token
def generate_token(username):
    token = jwt.encode({
        'user': username,
        'exp': datetime.datetime.utcnow() +
        datetime.timedelta(minutes=30)  # Token expires in 30
        minutes
    }, app.config['SECRET_KEY'], algorithm='HS256')
    return token

# Login route to obtain JWT
@app.route('/login', methods=['POST'])
def login():
    auth = request.json
    username = auth.get('username')
    password = auth.get('password')

    if username in users and users[username] == password:
        token = generate_token(username)
        return jsonify({'token': token}), 200
    return jsonify({'message': 'Invalid credentials'}), 401

# Protected route
@app.route('/protected', methods=['GET'])
def protected():
    token = request.headers.get('Authorization')
    if not token:
        return jsonify({'message': 'Token is missing!'}), 403

    try:
        data = jwt.decode(token, app.config['SECRET_KEY'],
        algorithms=['HS256'])
        return jsonify({'message': 'Protected route accessed!',
        'user': data['user']}), 200
    except jwt.ExpiredSignatureError:
        return jsonify({'message': 'Token has expired!'}), 403
    except jwt.InvalidTokenError:
        return jsonify({'message': 'Invalid token!'}), 403

if __name__ == '__main__':
```

```
app.run(debug=True)
```

In this example:

- Users log in and receive a JWT upon successful authentication.
- The JWT is then used to access protected routes in the API.

Protecting Endpoints with API Gateway

API Gateway acts as a crucial component in securing your Flask API deployed on AWS Lambda. It serves as a front door to your backend services, providing a single entry point for clients to interact with your API.

Key Features of API Gateway

1. **Authorization**: API Gateway supports various authorization methods, including AWS IAM roles, Lambda authorizers, and Amazon Cognito for user management. You can enforce authentication for your API endpoints, ensuring only authorized users can access protected resources.
2. **Request Validation**: API Gateway allows you to define request validation rules to ensure that incoming requests meet certain criteria. This helps prevent invalid requests from reaching your backend and enhances overall security.
3. **Throttling**: API Gateway can throttle incoming requests based on defined limits. Throttling helps protect your backend from sudden traffic spikes and potential denial-of-service attacks.
4. **CORS Support**: Cross-Origin Resource Sharing (CORS) is essential for APIs that will be accessed from web applications hosted on different domains. API Gateway allows you to configure CORS settings to enable secure cross-origin requests.
5. **Custom Domain Names**: You can configure custom domain names for your APIs, allowing for better branding and easier access.
6. **Monitoring and Logging**: API Gateway provides detailed logging and monitoring capabilities, allowing you to track usage patterns and

detect potential security issues.

Implementing Authorization with API Gateway

To protect your Flask API endpoints using API Gateway, you can implement various authorization methods, such as:

- **AWS IAM Roles**: Use AWS IAM to define policies that restrict access to your API based on user roles. This method is suitable for applications where AWS resources are accessed by other AWS services.
- **Lambda Authorizers**: Lambda authorizers allow you to create custom authentication and authorization logic using AWS Lambda. You can validate JWT tokens or perform other checks before granting access to your API.
- **Amazon Cognito**: Amazon Cognito provides user management and authentication features, allowing you to manage users and access tokens easily.

Here's a brief example of how to set up a Lambda authorizer in API Gateway:

1. **Create a Lambda Authorizer**: Write a Lambda function that validates incoming JWT tokens and returns an IAM policy that allows or denies access.
2. **Configure API Gateway**: In the API Gateway console, create a new authorizer and link it to your Lambda authorizer function.
3. **Attach the Authorizer to Routes**: When defining your API routes, attach the authorizer to the routes you want to protect.
4. **Deploy the API**: Deploy your changes to API Gateway, making the authorizer active for incoming requests.

By implementing API Gateway for authorization, you add an additional layer of security to your Flask API, ensuring that only authenticated users can access protected resources.

Rate Limiting and Throttling for Flask APIs

Rate limiting is a critical security feature for APIs, particularly in serverless environments where traffic can fluctuate significantly. By controlling the number of requests a user or client can make in a given timeframe, you can prevent abuse, protect your backend from excessive load, and ensure fair usage of resources.

Why Rate Limiting is Important

1. **Protecting Against Abuse**: Rate limiting helps prevent malicious users from overwhelming your API with excessive requests, which could lead to denial-of-service (DoS) attacks.
2. **Maintaining Performance**: By controlling request volume, you can ensure that your API remains responsive and available to legitimate users.
3. **Fair Usage**: Rate limiting ensures that no single user can monopolize resources, allowing for a more equitable distribution of access among all users.

Implementing Rate Limiting in Flask

To implement rate limiting in a Flask API, you can use the Flask-Limiter extension. This extension provides an easy way to add rate limiting to your API routes.

Example Code: Here's a basic example of how to use Flask-Limiter to add rate limiting to your Flask API:

```
python
Copy code
from flask import Flask, jsonify
from flask_limiter import Limiter
from flask_limiter.util import get_remote_address

app = Flask(__name__)
limiter = Limiter(get_remote_address, app=app)

@app.route('/api/data')
```

```python
@limiter.limit("5 per minute")  # Limit to 5 requests per minute
def get_data():
    return jsonify({"data": "This is some data!"})

if __name__ == '__main__':
    app.run(debug=True)
```

In this example:

- The @limiter.limit("5 per minute") decorator limits the /api/data route to five requests per minute per IP address. If a user exceeds this limit, they will receive a 429 Too Many Requests error.

You can customize the rate limit based on your API's requirements, such as applying different limits to different routes or user roles.

API Gateway Throttling

In addition to implementing rate limiting at the application level, AWS API Gateway provides built-in throttling features. API Gateway allows you to configure throttling limits for your API stages, including burst limits and steady-state limits.

- **Burst Limits**: The maximum number of requests that can be handled in a short period (e.g., 500 requests per second).
- **Steady-State Limits**: The average number of requests that can be handled over a longer timeframe (e.g., 100 requests per second).

To configure throttling in API Gateway:

1. Go to the API Gateway console and select your API.
2. Navigate to the "Stages" section and choose the stage you want to configure.
3. Under "Throttle", set your desired burst and steady-state limits.

By using both Flask-Limiter and API Gateway throttling, you can ensure that your Flask API remains responsive and secure under varying traffic conditions.

Securing Data with HTTPS and Cloudflare

Data security is paramount when developing APIs, especially those that handle sensitive user information. One of the key measures to protect data in transit is to use HTTPS, which encrypts communication between the client and the server.

Why Use HTTPS?

1. **Data Encryption**: HTTPS encrypts the data transmitted between the client and server, preventing eavesdropping and man-in-the-middle attacks.
2. **Data Integrity**: HTTPS ensures that the data sent and received has not been tampered with during transmission.
3. **Authentication**: HTTPS verifies the identity of the server, providing assurance to clients that they are communicating with the legitimate API endpoint.

Implementing HTTPS for Flask APIs

To secure your Flask API with HTTPS, you typically use a combination of AWS services and SSL/TLS certificates. Here's how to do it:

1. **Use AWS API Gateway**: When you deploy your Flask API to AWS Lambda through API Gateway, HTTPS is enabled by default for all API Gateway endpoints.
2. **Custom Domain Name**: If you want to use a custom domain name for your API, you can configure a custom domain name in API Gateway and associate it with your API. This process allows you to use HTTPS with your custom domain.
3. **SSL/TLS Certificates**: To use HTTPS with a custom domain, you need to obtain an SSL/TLS certificate. You can use AWS Certificate Manager (ACM) to provision and manage your certificates. AWS provides free SSL certificates that you can easily use with your custom domain.

Using Cloudflare for Additional Security

Cloudflare is a popular content delivery network (CDN) and security service that provides additional protection for your APIs. It offers several features that enhance API security, including:

1. **DDoS Protection**: Cloudflare protects your API from distributed denial-of-service (DDoS) attacks by filtering out malicious traffic before it reaches your server.
2. **Web Application Firewall (WAF)**: Cloudflare's WAF helps protect your API from common web vulnerabilities, such as SQL injection and cross-site scripting (XSS).
3. **Rate Limiting**: In addition to rate limiting in your Flask API, you can configure rate limiting at the Cloudflare level to protect against abuse and excessive requests.
4. **SSL/TLS Termination**: Cloudflare can manage SSL/TLS certificates, providing an additional layer of security for your API. You can configure your API to use HTTPS with Cloudflare while benefiting from their additional security features.

Setting Up Cloudflare

To use Cloudflare with your Flask API:

1. **Sign Up for Cloudflare**: Create a Cloudflare account and add your domain to their service.
2. **Update DNS Settings**: Change your domain's DNS settings to point to Cloudflare's nameservers.
3. **Configure SSL/TLS**: In the Cloudflare dashboard, configure the SSL/TLS settings. You can choose between Full (encrypts the connection between Cloudflare and your server) or Flexible (encrypts the connection between the user and Cloudflare but not between Cloudflare and your server).
4. **Enable Additional Security Features**: Configure rate limiting, WAF rules, and DDoS protection according to your needs.

In this chapter, we explored the critical aspects of securing Flask APIs in a serverless environment. We began by understanding the fundamentals of API security and then discussed the implementation of authentication using OAuth2 and JWT. We examined the protective measures provided by AWS API Gateway, including authorization, request validation, and throttling.

Furthermore, we covered the importance of securing data transmission using HTTPS and how to enhance API security with Cloudflare. By implementing these security measures, you can ensure that your Flask API is protected against unauthorized access and malicious attacks.

Chapter 5: Optimizing Flask API Performance in a Serverless Environment

Chapter 5: Optimizing Flask API Performance in a Serverless Environment

In the world of serverless architecture, performance optimization is essential for providing a responsive and efficient user experience. Flask, as a micro web framework, offers flexibility and simplicity, but developers must implement strategies to ensure their APIs perform optimally, especially when deployed in a serverless environment like AWS Lambda. This chapter will cover the various techniques and best practices for optimizing the performance of Flask APIs, focusing on caching, asynchronous processing, optimizing database interactions, minimizing cold starts, and monitoring API performance.

Understanding Performance Optimization in Serverless Architecture

Performance optimization involves improving the responsiveness, efficiency, and scalability of your application. In serverless architectures, where applications are often event-driven and stateless, optimization strategies may differ from traditional server-based applications. Factors affecting performance include execution time, cold start latency, resource allocation, and response times.

Key Metrics for API Performance

Before diving into optimization strategies, it's essential to understand the key metrics that reflect your API's performance:

Latency: The time it takes for an API request to be processed and the response to be returned. Lower latency is critical for providing a good user experience.

Throughput: The number of requests your API can handle per unit of time. Higher throughput indicates better performance and scalability.

Cold Start Time: The delay experienced when a serverless function is invoked for the first time or after a period of inactivity. Reducing cold start times is crucial for improving the responsiveness of your API.

Error Rates: The percentage of requests that result in errors. Monitoring error rates helps identify potential issues in your API.

Resource Utilization: The amount of memory and CPU resources used by your serverless functions. Optimizing resource utilization helps reduce costs and improve performance.

1. Caching Strategies for Flask APIs

Caching is one of the most effective techniques for optimizing API performance. By storing frequently accessed data in a cache, you can reduce the load on your backend and improve response times for users. There are several types of caching strategies that can be applied to Flask APIs:

A. HTTP Caching

HTTP caching allows responses from your API to be stored temporarily by clients or intermediate servers. This reduces the need to repeatedly fetch the same data from the server.

Cache-Control Headers: You can use HTTP headers to control caching behavior. For example, the Cache-Control header can specify how long a response should be cached. Here's how to set cache headers in a Flask route:

python

Copy code

```
from flask import Flask, jsonify, make_response

app = Flask(__name__)
```

@app.route('/api/data')

def get_data():

response = make_response(jsonify({"data": "This is cached data!"}))

response.headers['Cache-Control'] = 'public, max-age=300' # Cache for 5 minutes

return response

ETags: ETags (Entity Tags) are used for conditional requests. When a client requests a resource, the server can return an ETag header that represents the current version of the resource. If the client has the latest version cached, it can avoid fetching the resource again.

B. In-Memory Caching

In-memory caching stores data in memory for quick access, reducing the need for database queries and improving response times. Two popular in-memory caching solutions are Redis and Memcached.

Redis: Redis is an open-source in-memory data structure store that supports various data types. You can use Redis to cache API responses, user sessions, or other frequently accessed data.

Flask-Caching: The Flask-Caching extension makes it easy to integrate caching into your Flask applications. Here's how to set it up with Redis:

python

Copy code

from flask import Flask, jsonify

```
from flask_caching import Cache
```

app = Flask(__name__)

```
cache = Cache(app, config={'CACHE_TYPE': 'redis'})
```

@cache.cached(timeout=60, query_string=True)

@app.route('/api/data')

def get_data():

return jsonify({"data": "This is cached data from Redis!"})

In this example, the @cache.cached decorator caches the response for 60 seconds, significantly improving performance for repeated requests.

C. Database Query Caching

In addition to caching API responses, consider caching database queries. If your application frequently retrieves the same data from a database, caching the results can reduce database load and improve performance.

Flask-SQLAlchemy: If you are using Flask-SQLAlchemy, you can implement query caching by using SQLAlchemy's built-in caching capabilities or by combining Flask-Caching with SQLAlchemy.

2. Asynchronous Processing in Flask

In a serverless environment, long-running tasks can lead to performance bottlenecks. Asynchronous processing allows you to offload time-consuming tasks from your API, enabling your Flask application to respond quickly to user requests.

A. Using Background Workers

For tasks that require significant processing time, consider using background workers to handle these tasks outside the request-response cycle. Background workers can be implemented using solutions like **Celery**, which allows you to run tasks asynchronously.

Install Celery:

bash

Copy code

pip install celery

Set Up Celery in Your Flask Application:

python

Copy code

from flask import Flask, jsonify

```
from celery import Celery
```

app = Flask(__name__)

app.config['CELERY_BROKER_URL'] = 'redis://localhost:6379/0' # Using Redis as a message broker

```
celery = Celery(app.name, broker=app.config['CELERY_BROKER_URL'])
```

@celery.task

def long_running_task(data):

Simulate a long-running task

import time

time.sleep(10)

```
return f"Processed data: {data}"
```

@app.route('/api/process/<data>')

def process(data):

task = long_running_task.apply_async(args=[data])

return jsonify({"task_id": task.id}), 202

In this example, the long_running_task function is executed asynchronously, allowing the Flask API to respond quickly to the user while the task runs in the background.

Check Task Status:

You can implement an endpoint to check the status of the long-running task using Celery's built-in task status tracking.
   B. Asynchronous Requests
   If you need to make external API calls or perform other I/O-bound tasks, consider using asynchronous libraries such as aiohttp or httpx. Flask can be made asynchronous using the quart framework, which is built on top of Flask and supports asynchronous programming.
   Here's a brief example of making asynchronous HTTP requests:

python

Copy code

from quart import Quart, jsonify

```
import httpx

app = Quart(__name__)
```

@app.route('/api/fetch-data')

```
async def fetch_data():

    async with httpx.AsyncClient() as client:

        response = await client.get('https://api.example.com/data')

    return jsonify(response.json())
```

Using asynchronous requests improves the overall responsiveness of your API by allowing concurrent processing of I/O-bound tasks.

3. Optimizing Database Interactions

Database interactions can become a significant bottleneck in API performance. To optimize your Flask API's database interactions, consider the following strategies:

A. Connection Pooling

Connection pooling allows multiple requests to share a pool of database connections, reducing the overhead of establishing new connections for each request. If you are using Flask-SQLAlchemy, you can easily configure connection pooling by adjusting the settings in your database URI.

python

Copy code

```
app.config['SQLALCHEMY_DATABASE_URI'] = 'mysql+pymysql://user:password@localhost/dbname'

app.config['SQLALCHEMY_ENGINE_OPTIONS'] = {

    'pool_size': 10,
```

'max_overflow': 20,

'pool_timeout': 30,

}

This configuration sets up a connection pool with a maximum of 10 connections, allowing for efficient reuse of database connections.

B. Query Optimization

Optimizing your database queries can significantly improve performance. Consider the following practices:

Use Indexing: Indexing can improve query performance by reducing the amount of data scanned during query execution. Analyze slow queries and create appropriate indexes on columns used in WHERE clauses, JOINs, and ORDER BY clauses.

Limit Data Retrieval: Retrieve only the data you need by using the LIMIT clause or selecting specific columns instead of fetching entire rows.

Batch Queries: If your application needs to perform multiple queries, consider batching them into a single query when possible. This reduces the number of round trips to the database.

Use ORM Effectively: If using an Object-Relational Mapper (ORM) like SQLAlchemy, make sure to use it effectively. Utilize lazy loading and eager loading appropriately to optimize data retrieval.

C. Caching Database Queries

In addition to connection pooling, consider caching the results of frequently executed database queries. This reduces the load on your database and improves response times.

Here's an example of how to implement query caching with Flask-Caching:

python

Copy code

from flask import Flask, jsonify

from flask_sqlalchemy import SQLAlchemy

```
from flask_caching import Cache
```

app = Flask(__name__)

*app.config['SQLALCHEMY_DATABASE_URI'] =
'mysql+pymysql://user:password@localhost/dbname'*

```
cache = Cache(app, config={'CACHE_TYPE': 'redis'})

db = SQLAlchemy(app)
```

class User(db.Model):

id = db.Column(db.Integer, primary_key=True)

```
username = db.Column(db.String(80), unique=True, nullable=False)
```

@app.route('/api/users/<int:user_id>')

@cache.cached(timeout=60) # Cache the result for 60 seconds

def get_user(user_id):

user = User.query.get(user_id)

if user:

return jsonify({"id": user.id, "username": user.username}) return jsonify({"message": "User not found"}), 404

In this example, the @cache.cached decorator caches the response for user retrieval, significantly improving performance for repeated requests.

4. Minimizing Cold Starts

Cold starts are a common challenge in serverless architectures, especially for AWS Lambda. When a Lambda function is invoked for the first time after a period of inactivity, AWS must spin up a new execution environment, leading to increased latency.

A. Use Provisioned Concurrency

AWS Lambda offers a feature called **Provisioned Concurrency**, which allows you to keep a specific number of instances of your function warm at all times. This reduces cold start latency for your API.

To configure Provisioned Concurrency:

Go to the AWS Lambda console and select your function.

Navigate to the "Configuration" tab and find the "Concurrency" section.

Set the number of provisioned concurrent instances you want to maintain.

Provisioned Concurrency is particularly useful for APIs that require consistent low latency, such as those serving front-end applications or real-time services.

B. Optimize Function Initialization

The cold start time can also be affected by the initialization code in your Lambda function. To minimize cold starts, consider the following practices:

Reduce Package Size: Keep your function package size as small as possible. Avoid including unnecessary libraries and assets. Use tools like pipreqs to generate a requirements.txt file that only includes the dependencies you need.

Minimize Initialization Logic: Avoid complex initialization logic in your Lambda function. Move any heavy computation or resource-intensive tasks out of the global scope of your function. Instead, initialize resources only when they are needed within the function.

Use Lightweight Libraries: If possible, choose lightweight libraries to reduce the overhead during function initialization. This can help speed up cold start times.

5. Monitoring API Performance in AWS CloudWatch

Monitoring is crucial for maintaining the performance of your Flask API in a serverless environment. AWS CloudWatch provides comprehensive monitoring and logging capabilities for AWS Lambda and API Gateway.

A. Setting Up CloudWatch Monitoring

Enable CloudWatch Metrics: By default, AWS Lambda publishes various metrics to CloudWatch, including invocation count, error rates, duration, and throttles. You can view these metrics in the CloudWatch console.

Create Custom Metrics: If you want to track additional performance indicators, you can create custom metrics using the CloudWatch SDK. This allows you to monitor specific application performance metrics relevant to your use case.

CloudWatch Alarms: Set up CloudWatch alarms to notify you when certain thresholds are exceeded. For example, you can create alarms for high error rates or increased response times, allowing you to proactively address performance issues.

B. Analyzing Logs

In addition to metrics, CloudWatch Logs provides valuable insights into the behavior of your Lambda functions. You can view detailed logs of function executions, including any logging statements you've added to your code.

Using CloudWatch Logs: When you deploy your Flask API to AWS Lambda, AWS automatically creates a log group for your function. You can view the logs in the CloudWatch console or use the AWS CLI to retrieve them.

Debugging with Logs: Use logging to capture critical information about requests and responses, including any errors that occur during execution. Proper logging can help you identify and troubleshoot performance bottlenecks and other issues.

Conclusion

In this chapter, we explored various techniques for optimizing the performance of Flask APIs deployed in a serverless environment. We began by understanding the importance of performance optimization and the key metrics to monitor.

We discussed caching strategies, including HTTP caching, in-memory caching with Redis, and query caching to reduce load on your backend. Asynchronous processing techniques were introduced, emphasizing the use of background workers and asynchronous requests to offload long-running tasks.

Database interaction optimization was also covered, focusing on connection pooling, query optimization, and caching database queries. Additionally, we examined strategies for minimizing cold starts, including the use of Provisioned Concurrency and optimizing function initialization.

Finally, we highlighted the importance of monitoring API performance using AWS CloudWatch, including setting up metrics, analyzing logs, and creating alarms for proactive performance management.

By implementing these optimization strategies, you can ensure that your Flask API is not only scalable but also provides a fast and responsive experience for users. In the next chapter, we will delve into the topic of securing your Flask APIs, covering authentication, authorization, and data protection strategies to safeguard your application against various threats.

4o mini

You said:

write in 7000 words Chapter 6

ChatGPT said:
ChatGPT

Chapter 6: Handling Increased Traffic with Flask APIs in a Serverless Environment

As your Flask APIs gain popularity, the ability to handle increased traffic efficiently becomes paramount. In a serverless environment like AWS Lambda, scalability is built-in, but developers must implement strategies to ensure that APIs can accommodate varying levels of demand without degrading performance. This chapter will explore various approaches to effectively manage increased traffic, focusing on optimizing resource usage, implementing asynchronous processing, leveraging load balancing, and ensuring fault tolerance. We will also discuss strategies for improving response times and overall user experience.

1. Understanding Increased Traffic and Its Implications

When an API experiences increased traffic, several challenges can arise, including:

Resource Exhaustion: A sudden spike in traffic can lead to excessive resource consumption, resulting in throttling or degraded performance.

Increased Latency: As more requests are processed, response times can increase if the backend cannot keep up with demand.

Error Rates: High traffic volumes can lead to increased error rates, especially if rate limiting and throttling are not implemented effectively.

Service Availability: In extreme cases, sudden spikes in traffic can lead to service outages if not managed properly.

Understanding these implications is crucial for implementing effective strategies to handle increased traffic.

2. Optimizing Resource Usage in AWS Lambda

AWS Lambda automatically manages scaling, but there are still several best practices to optimize resource usage and ensure that your Flask APIs can handle increased traffic effectively.

A. Configuring Memory and Timeout Settings

Lambda functions can be configured with different memory allocations and timeout settings, both of which affect performance.

Memory Allocation: AWS Lambda allows you to allocate between 128 MB and 10 GB of memory to your functions. Increasing the memory allocation not only provides more resources for your code but also increases CPU allocation, which can lead to improved performance. Test your API under different memory configurations to find the optimal setting.

Timeout Settings: The maximum execution timeout for AWS Lambda is 15 minutes. Setting an appropriate timeout based on the expected duration of your API calls is important to prevent premature termination. Adjust your timeout settings in the zappa_settings.json file for Zappa deployments.

B. Provisioning Concurrency

Provisioned Concurrency is a feature that allows you to pre-warm a specific number of Lambda instances to reduce cold start latency and ensure that your API can handle sudden traffic spikes.

Use Cases: Provisioned Concurrency is particularly useful for APIs that experience predictable traffic patterns, such as during promotional events or product launches.

To configure Provisioned Concurrency:

Navigate to the AWS Lambda console and select your function.

Click on the "Configuration" tab and scroll down to "Concurrency."

Set the number of provisioned concurrent instances that you want to maintain.

C. Monitoring and Adjusting Resource Usage

AWS CloudWatch provides monitoring capabilities that allow you to track key performance metrics for your Lambda functions. Regularly monitoring these metrics will help you identify trends and adjust resource usage accordingly.

Analyze Invocation Metrics: Monitor the number of invocations and response times. If you notice an increase in invocations coupled with high latency, consider increasing memory allocation or configuring Provisioned Concurrency.

Evaluate Throttle Events: Keep an eye on the number of throttle events to understand if your function is being overwhelmed. If you encounter throttling, consider adjusting concurrency limits or optimizing your code for better performance.

Implementing Asynchronous Processing

Asynchronous processing can significantly enhance your API's ability to handle increased traffic by offloading long-running tasks from the main request-response cycle. This allows your Flask API to remain responsive and deliver a better user experience.

   A. Using Background Workers

   Background workers, such as those provided by Celery, enable you to offload resource-intensive tasks, allowing your API to quickly respond to user requests.

Install Celery:

bash

Copy code

pip install celery

Configure Celery with Flask: Here's an example of how to set up Celery with Flask:

python

Copy code

from flask import Flask, jsonify

```
from celery import Celery
```

app = Flask(__name__)

app.config['CELERY_BROKER_URL'] = 'redis://localhost:6379/0' # Using Redis as a message broker

```
celery = Celery(app.name, broker=app.config['CELERY_BROKER_URL'])
```

@celery.task

def long_running_task(data):

import time

time.sleep(10) # Simulate a long-running task

```
return f"Processed data: {data}"
```

@app.route('/api/process/<data>')

def process(data):

task = long_running_task.apply_async(args=[data])

```
return jsonify({"task_id": task.id}), 202
```

if __name__ == '__main__':

app.run(debug=True)

In this example, the long_running_task function simulates a time-consuming task. When a request is made to the /api/process/<data> endpoint, the task is executed asynchronously, allowing the API to respond immediately.

Check Task Status: *You can implement an endpoint to check the status of long-running tasks using Celery's built-in task tracking.*

B. Using Asynchronous Libraries

If your application needs to handle I/O-bound tasks, consider using asynchronous libraries like httpx or aiohttp for making concurrent HTTP requests. This approach can enhance performance by allowing your Flask API to make multiple requests without blocking.

Example using httpx:

python

Copy code

```
from quart import Quart, jsonify
import httpx

app = Quart(__name__)


@app.route('/api/fetch-data')
async def fetch_data():
    async with httpx.AsyncClient() as client:
        response = await client.get('https://api.example.com/data')
    return jsonify(response.json())


if __name__ == '__main__':
    app.run()
```

By implementing asynchronous processing, you can effectively handle increased traffic while maintaining responsive user interactions.

4. Leveraging Load Balancing

While AWS Lambda automatically manages scaling, load balancing is still an essential consideration for Flask APIs, especially when multiple functions or services are involved.

A. Understanding Load Balancing

Load balancing distributes incoming requests across multiple server instances to ensure that no single instance is overwhelmed. In a serverless environment, AWS automatically handles load balancing for Lambda functions, but there are still strategies to optimize performance.

B. API Gateway as a Load Balancer

AWS API Gateway acts as a load balancer for your Flask API by routing incoming requests to the appropriate Lambda functions. This allows you to handle traffic efficiently, even if multiple endpoints are being accessed simultaneously.

Define Throttling Policies: Use API Gateway's throttling capabilities to control the rate of incoming requests. This helps protect your backend from sudden traffic spikes and ensures availability.

Custom Domain Names: If using custom domain names with API Gateway, ensure that DNS settings are properly configured to distribute traffic effectively.

5. Ensuring Fault Tolerance

Fault tolerance is crucial for maintaining API availability, especially during periods of increased traffic. Implementing strategies to handle failures gracefully will improve user experience and maintain service reliability.

A. Implementing Retry Logic

In a serverless environment, transient errors can occur due to resource availability or network issues. Implementing retry logic in your Flask API can help mitigate the impact of these errors.

Use AWS SDK Retry Mechanism: If your Flask API makes calls to other AWS services (e.g., DynamoDB, S3), utilize the built-in retry mechanisms provided by the AWS SDK to automatically retry failed requests.

Custom Retry Logic: For external API calls, implement custom retry logic using libraries such as tenacity:

bash

Copy code

pip install tenacity

Example usage:

python

Copy code

```
from tenacity import retry, stop_after_attempt, wait_fixed
```

@retry(stop=stop_after_attempt(3), wait=wait_fixed(2))

def make_external_request():

 # Logic to make an external API call

In this example, the function will retry up to three times, waiting two seconds between attempts, if it encounters errors.

B. Circuit Breaker Pattern

The circuit breaker pattern is a fault tolerance design pattern that prevents an application from making calls to a service that is likely to fail. It allows you to manage failures gracefully and avoid cascading failures across services.

Implement Circuit Breakers: Use libraries like pybreaker to implement circuit breakers in your Flask API. This pattern helps ensure that your application does not overwhelm failing services, allowing them to recover.

Example usage:

bash

Copy code

pip install pybreaker

python

Copy code

```
import pybreaker

circuit_breaker = pybreaker.CircuitBreaker(failure_threshold=3, recovery_timeout=10)
```

@circuit_breaker

def make_external_request():

 # Logic to make an external API call

In this example, if three consecutive failures occur, the circuit breaker will open, preventing further calls to the external service for a specified recovery timeout period.

  6. Improving Response Times

Reducing response times is critical for enhancing user experience and ensuring that your Flask API can handle increased traffic effectively. Here are some strategies to consider:

  A. Optimize Function Code

Minimize Initialization Code: Reduce the amount of initialization code that runs when the Lambda function is invoked. Keep initialization logic to a minimum to decrease cold start times.

Use Lightweight Libraries: If possible, choose lightweight libraries to reduce the overhead during function execution.

Profile and Optimize Code: Use profiling tools to identify performance bottlenecks in your code. Optimize slow functions and minimize processing time wherever possible.

B. Use Content Delivery Networks (CDNs)

Using a CDN can improve response times by caching content closer to users. Cloudflare, AWS CloudFront, and other CDNs can help deliver static assets, API responses, and other content faster.

Cache API Responses: Configure your CDN to cache responses from your API. This reduces the load on your backend and speeds up response times for frequently accessed data.

Global Distribution: CDNs have a network of servers around the world, allowing users to access content from a nearby server, reducing latency.

7. Monitoring and Continuous Improvement

Monitoring is an ongoing process that helps you maintain the performance and reliability of your Flask API. Regularly reviewing metrics and performance data allows you to make informed decisions about scaling, optimizing, and enhancing your API.

A. Setting Up CloudWatch Dashboards

Create CloudWatch dashboards to visualize key performance metrics for your Flask API, including:

Invocation count

Duration

Error rates

Throttle rates

By setting up a dashboard, you can quickly identify trends and anomalies in your API's performance.
   B. Conducting Load Testing
   Load testing simulates high levels of traffic to your API, helping you identify potential bottlenecks and performance issues before they occur in production. Use tools like **Apache JMeter**, **Artillery**, or **Gatling** to conduct load tests and analyze your API's performance under stress.

Define Test Scenarios: Create scenarios that mimic real-world usage patterns, including peak traffic periods and common user actions.

Analyze Results: After conducting load tests, analyze the results to identify any performance issues, such as increased response times or error rates.

Iterate and Optimize: Use the insights gained from load testing to refine your API and optimize performance. Regularly conduct load tests as your application evolves.

Conclusion

In this chapter, we explored the essential strategies for handling increased traffic with Flask APIs in a serverless environment. We began by understanding the implications of increased traffic and the importance of optimizing resource usage in AWS Lambda.

We discussed implementing asynchronous processing, leveraging load balancing, and ensuring fault tolerance through techniques like retry logic and circuit breakers. Additionally, we covered methods for improving response times, such as optimizing function code and utilizing content delivery networks (CDNs).

Finally, we emphasized the importance of monitoring and continuous improvement to maintain the performance and reliability of your Flask API. By applying these strategies, you can ensure that your serverless Flask API is equipped to handle traffic spikes while providing a responsive user experience.

Chapter 6: Integrating Third-Party Services and APIs with Flask

Integrating third-party services and APIs into your Flask applications can significantly enhance functionality, providing additional features and resources without the need to build everything from scratch. In this chapter, we will explore various aspects of integrating third-party services, focusing on API design principles, popular third-party services, authentication methods, error handling, and best practices for creating robust integrations. We will also include practical examples to demonstrate how to effectively integrate these services into your Flask APIs.

1. Understanding API Integration

API integration involves connecting your application with external services or platforms via their application programming interfaces (APIs). This can involve retrieving data, sending requests, or leveraging the functionality provided by the third-party service.

A. Benefits of API Integration

1. **Enhanced Functionality**: By integrating third-party services, you can add powerful features without having to develop them in-house. For example, you might integrate payment processing, geolocation, or data storage services.
2. **Reduced Development Time**: Leveraging existing services can

accelerate development timelines, allowing you to focus on your core application logic rather than reinventing the wheel.
3. **Access to Expertise**: Third-party services often specialize in specific domains (e.g., payments, messaging, analytics). Integrating these services allows you to leverage their expertise and infrastructure.
4. **Scalability**: Many third-party services are built to scale, meaning you can handle growth without worrying about the underlying infrastructure.

B. Considerations for API Integration

While integrating third-party services offers many benefits, several considerations should be kept in mind:

1. **Security**: Ensure that the third-party service is secure and complies with relevant regulations (e.g., GDPR, PCI DSS for payment processing). Use secure authentication methods to protect user data.
2. **Latency**: Integrating with external APIs can introduce latency, affecting your application's performance. Optimize how and when you make API calls to mitigate this issue.
3. **Error Handling**: External services may experience downtime or return errors. Implement robust error handling to manage these situations gracefully.
4. **Versioning**: APIs can change over time. Be mindful of versioning and ensure your application can handle updates or changes to the third-party service.

2. Common Third-Party Services for Flask APIs

There are numerous third-party services available that can be integrated into Flask APIs. Below are some popular categories and examples of services commonly used:

A. Payment Processing

Integrating payment processing services allows you to handle transactions securely and efficiently. Popular options include:

CHAPTER 6: INTEGRATING THIRD-PARTY SERVICES AND APIS WITH...

- **Stripe**: A widely used payment processor that provides APIs for handling payments, subscriptions, and invoicing. Stripe's API is known for its comprehensive documentation and ease of use.
- **PayPal**: PayPal offers APIs for processing payments and managing transactions, making it a popular choice for e-commerce applications.
- **Square**: Square provides APIs for payment processing, point-of-sale solutions, and customer management.

Example of Integrating Stripe: To integrate Stripe into your Flask API:

1. **Install Stripe SDK**:

```bash
Copy code
pip install stripe
```

1. **Create a Payment Intent**:

```python
Copy code
from flask import Flask, request, jsonify
import stripe

app = Flask(__name__)
stripe.api_key = 'your_secret_key'

@app.route('/api/create-payment-intent', methods=['POST'])
def create_payment_intent():
    data = request.json
    amount = data.get('amount')  # Amount in cents

    try:
```

```
        intent = stripe.PaymentIntent.create(
            amount=amount,
            currency='usd',
        )
        return jsonify({"client_secret":
intent['client_secret']}), 200
    except Exception as e:
        return jsonify({"error": str(e)}), 400
```

In this example, the /api/create-payment-intent endpoint creates a payment intent using Stripe's API, returning the client_secret to the client for processing the payment.

B. Authentication Services

Integrating authentication services allows you to manage user authentication and authorization securely. Some popular options include:

- **Auth0**: A flexible authentication and authorization platform that provides SDKs and APIs for integrating various authentication methods (social, enterprise, etc.).
- **Firebase Authentication**: A service that provides authentication for web and mobile applications, supporting email/password and social media sign-ins.
- **Okta**: A cloud-based identity management service that provides authentication and authorization features.

Example of Integrating Auth0: To integrate Auth0 into your Flask API:

1. **Install Auth0 SDK**:

```bash
Copy code
pip install auth0-python
```

CHAPTER 6: INTEGRATING THIRD-PARTY SERVICES AND APIS WITH...

1. **Verify JWT Tokens**:

```python
Copy code
from flask import Flask, request, jsonify
from functools import wraps
from jose import jwt

app = Flask(__name__)

AUTH0_DOMAIN = 'your-auth0-domain'
API_IDENTIFIER = 'your-api-identifier'
ALGORITHMS = ['RS256']

def requires_auth(f):
    @wraps(f)
    def decorated(*args, **kwargs):
        token = request.headers.get('Authorization', None)
        if not token:
            return jsonify({"message": "Missing token"}), 401

        try:
            payload = jwt.decode(token.split()[1],
                options={"verify_signature": False})  # Decoding
                without verification for demonstration
            return f(*args, **kwargs)
        except jwt.ExpiredSignatureError:
            return jsonify({"message": "Token expired"}), 401
        except jwt.JWTClaimsError:
            return jsonify({"message": "Invalid claims"}), 401
        except Exception:
            return jsonify({"message": "Invalid token"}), 401

    return decorated

@app.route('/api/protected', methods=['GET'])
@requires_auth
def protected():
    return jsonify({"message": "You have accessed a protected
```

```
    route!"}), 200

if __name__ == '__main__':
    app.run(debug=True)
```

In this example, the requires_auth decorator verifies the JWT token issued by Auth0, allowing access to the protected route only if the token is valid.

C. Messaging and Communication Services

Integrating messaging services can enhance user engagement and communication within your application. Popular options include:

- **Twilio**: A cloud communications platform that provides APIs for sending SMS, making phone calls, and managing communication workflows.
- **SendGrid**: An email delivery service that offers APIs for sending transactional and marketing emails.
- **Slack API**: A messaging platform API that allows you to send messages, notifications, and alerts to Slack channels.

Example of Integrating Twilio: To integrate Twilio for sending SMS:

1. **Install Twilio SDK**:

```bash
Copy code
pip install twilio
```

1. **Send an SMS**:

CHAPTER 6: INTEGRATING THIRD-PARTY SERVICES AND APIS WITH...

```python
Copy code
from flask import Flask, request, jsonify
from twilio.rest import Client

app = Flask(__name__)
twilio_client = Client('your_account_sid', 'your_auth_token')

@app.route('/api/send-sms', methods=['POST'])
def send_sms():
    data = request.json
    message = twilio_client.messages.create(
        body=data.get('message'),
        from_='your_twilio_phone_number',
        to=data.get('to')
    )
    return jsonify({"sid": message.sid}), 200

if __name__ == '__main__':
    app.run(debug=True)
```

In this example, the /api/send-sms endpoint sends an SMS using the Twilio API, returning the message SID to confirm delivery.

3. Authentication and Security in API Integrations

When integrating third-party services, it's essential to implement secure authentication mechanisms to protect sensitive data and ensure that only authorized users can access the API.

A. OAuth2 for Third-Party Integrations

Many third-party services use OAuth2 for authentication and authorization. OAuth2 provides a secure way for applications to access resources on behalf of users without exposing their credentials.

1. **Authorization Code Grant**: This is the most common flow for web applications. Users authenticate with the third-party service and grant permission for your application to access their data. The service then issues an authorization code that your application can exchange for access and refresh tokens.

2. **Implicit Grant**: This flow is used for client-side applications. Users authenticate with the service, and the service issues an access token directly to the application.
3. **Client Credentials Grant**: This flow is suitable for server-to-server communications, where the client application needs to access resources on behalf of itself, not on behalf of users.

Example of OAuth2 Integration: To integrate OAuth2 in your Flask API:

- Register your application with the third-party service to obtain a client ID and client secret.
- Implement the OAuth2 flow in your Flask API, handling the redirection and token exchange.

B. Securing API Keys and Secrets

When integrating with third-party services, you will often need to use API keys or secrets. It's crucial to store these securely to prevent unauthorized access.

1. **Environment Variables**: Store sensitive information such as API keys and secrets in environment variables. You can access these variables in your Flask application using os.environ.

```python
Copy code
import os

TWILIO_SID = os.environ.get('TWILIO_SID')
TWILIO_AUTH_TOKEN = os.environ.get('TWILIO_AUTH_TOKEN')
```

1. **Configuration Files**: Alternatively, you can use configuration files (e.g., .env files) to store sensitive information. Libraries like python-

CHAPTER 6: INTEGRATING THIRD-PARTY SERVICES AND APIS WITH...

dotenv can help load environment variables from these files.

2. **Secret Management Services**: Consider using secret management services like AWS Secrets Manager or HashiCorp Vault to manage sensitive information securely. These services provide APIs for securely accessing secrets in your application.

4. Error Handling in API Integrations

Integrating third-party services introduces the potential for errors, such as network issues, timeouts, or service outages. Implementing robust error handling is essential to ensure that your Flask API can gracefully handle these scenarios.

A. Graceful Error Handling

When integrating with external APIs, always anticipate that errors may occur. Implement error handling that provides meaningful feedback to users without exposing sensitive information.

1. **Try-Except Blocks**: Use try-except blocks to catch exceptions when making API calls. This allows you to handle specific exceptions gracefully.

```python
Copy code
@app.route('/api/send-sms', methods=['POST'])
def send_sms():
    data = request.json
    try:
        message = twilio_client.messages.create(
            body=data.get('message'),
            from_='your_twilio_phone_number',
            to=data.get('to')
        )
        return jsonify({"sid": message.sid}), 200
    except Exception as e:
        return jsonify({"error": str(e)}), 500
```

1. **Custom Error Messages**: Provide custom error messages that inform users of the issue without exposing sensitive details. For example, instead of returning a raw error message, you could return a user-friendly message.
2. **Logging Errors**: Log errors for later review and analysis. Use a logging library like Python's built-in logging module to log error details.

B. Handling Specific Error Codes

When integrating with third-party services, pay attention to the specific error codes returned by the API. Each service may have its own set of error codes, and handling these appropriately can enhance the user experience.

- **Rate Limiting Errors**: Many APIs enforce rate limits, returning error codes when limits are exceeded (e.g., HTTP 429). Implement logic to handle these errors, such as retrying after a delay or informing users to slow down their requests.
- **Authentication Errors**: If the authentication token is invalid or expired, handle these errors by prompting users to re-authenticate.
- **Service Unavailability**: When a third-party service is down, return a user-friendly message indicating that the service is temporarily unavailable.

5. Best Practices for Integrating Third-Party APIs

To ensure successful and efficient integration of third-party APIs, follow these best practices:

A. Read API Documentation

Before integrating with any third-party service, thoroughly read the API documentation. Understanding the available endpoints, request/response formats, authentication methods, and rate limits will help you design your integration effectively.

B. Use SDKs and Libraries

Many third-party services provide SDKs and libraries that simplify integration. These libraries often handle authentication, error handling, and

API calls, allowing you to focus on your application logic.

C. Implement Caching

To reduce the number of API calls and improve performance, consider implementing caching for responses from third-party APIs. This is especially useful for data that does not change frequently.

```python
Copy code
@app.route('/api/user/<int:user_id>')
@cache.cached(timeout=300)  # Cache for 5 minutes
def get_user(user_id):
    # Call to an external API to get user data
```

D. Monitor API Usage

Keep track of how often you are calling third-party APIs and the associated costs. Many services charge based on usage, so monitoring can help you manage costs effectively.

- **Set Usage Alerts**: Some APIs allow you to set usage alerts or limits to avoid exceeding quotas.

E. Version Control

APIs can change over time, leading to potential issues with your integrations. Keep track of the version of the API you are using and stay informed about any upcoming changes or deprecations.

6. Case Studies of Flask API Integrations

To illustrate the concepts discussed in this chapter, let's explore a few case studies that showcase the integration of third-party services with Flask APIs.

Case Study 1: E-Commerce Application with Stripe

Scenario: An e-commerce application requires payment processing capabilities. The developers decide to integrate Stripe to handle transactions.

Integration Steps:

1. **Set Up Stripe Account**: The developers create a Stripe account and

obtain the necessary API keys.
2. **Implement Payment Processing**: They create an endpoint for processing payments using the Stripe API, handling payment intents and confirmations.
3. **Error Handling**: The application includes error handling for potential issues such as card declines and API errors.
4. **Testing**: Thorough testing is performed in Stripe's test environment before going live.

Case Study 2: User Authentication with Auth0
Scenario: A Flask application requires user authentication and authorization. The team decides to integrate Auth0 for managing user accounts.
Integration Steps:

1. **Create Auth0 Application**: The developers set up an application in Auth0 and configure allowed callback URLs.
2. **Implement Authentication Flow**: They implement the authentication flow, including redirecting users to Auth0 for login and handling callback responses.
3. **Securing Routes**: The application secures protected routes by implementing JWT verification.
4. **User Roles and Permissions**: They manage user roles and permissions within Auth0 to control access to different parts of the application.

Case Study 3: SMS Notifications with Twilio
Scenario: A messaging platform needs to send SMS notifications to users. The developers choose to integrate Twilio for SMS delivery.
Integration Steps:

1. **Sign Up for Twilio**: The team creates a Twilio account and obtains API credentials.
2. **Implement SMS Sending**: They create an endpoint for sending SMS messages, handling both success and error responses.

3. **Rate Limiting**: The application implements rate limiting to control the number of SMS messages sent to prevent abuse.
4. **Monitoring**: The team monitors SMS delivery rates and logs any issues for further analysis.

Conclusion

In this chapter, we explored the essential aspects of integrating third-party services and APIs into Flask applications. We began by understanding the benefits and considerations of API integration, discussing popular services such as payment processing, authentication, and messaging.

We covered key strategies for implementing secure authentication, error handling, and best practices for successful integrations. Through practical examples, we illustrated how to leverage third-party services effectively while maintaining robust application performance and security.

Chapter 7: Testing Flask APIs: Strategies and Best Practices

Testing is a crucial aspect of software development, ensuring that your Flask APIs function as intended, are reliable, and provide a positive user experience. In this chapter, we will explore various strategies and best practices for testing Flask APIs, including unit testing, integration testing, end-to-end testing, and performance testing. We will also discuss the tools and frameworks available for testing, along with real-world examples to illustrate how to effectively implement testing in your Flask applications.

1. The Importance of Testing APIs

Testing APIs is essential for several reasons:

- **Ensures Functionality**: Thorough testing verifies that the API endpoints behave as expected, returning the correct responses for valid requests and appropriate error messages for invalid requests.
- **Identifies Bugs Early**: Implementing a robust testing strategy helps identify bugs and issues early in the development process, reducing the cost and effort required to fix them.
- **Enhances Security**: Testing helps identify vulnerabilities and security weaknesses in your API, allowing you to address potential risks before they are exploited.

- **Facilitates Continuous Integration/Continuous Deployment (CI/CD)**: Automated tests enable teams to adopt CI/CD practices, ensuring that changes to the codebase do not introduce new bugs and that the application remains stable.
- **Improves User Experience**: By ensuring that the API performs reliably, testing contributes to a better overall user experience, increasing user satisfaction and trust in the application.

2. Types of Testing for Flask APIs

Flask APIs can be subjected to several types of testing, each serving a specific purpose:

A. Unit Testing

Unit testing focuses on testing individual components or functions in isolation. In the context of Flask APIs, this often involves testing specific routes or helper functions to ensure they return the expected results.

Key Characteristics:

- Tests individual units of code (e.g., functions, methods).
- Typically performed using testing frameworks such as unittest or pytest.
- Fast execution time, allowing for quick feedback during development.

Example of Unit Testing with pytest: Here's an example of how to set up unit tests for a Flask API using pytest:

1. **Install pytest**:

```bash
Copy code
pip install pytest
```

1. **Create a Test File** (e.g., test_app.py):

```python
Copy code
import pytest
from app import app  # Import your Flask application

@pytest.fixture
def client():
    with app.test_client() as client:
        yield client

def test_home_page(client):
    response = client.get('/')
    assert response.status_code == 200
    assert b'Welcome to your first serverless Flask API!' in response.data

def test_get_data(client):
    response = client.get('/api/data')
    assert response.status_code == 200
    assert response.json == {"data": "This is some data!"}
```

In this example, we use pytest fixtures to create a test client for our Flask application. The test_home_page and test_get_data functions verify the responses for specific routes.

B. Integration Testing

Integration testing involves testing how different components of the application work together. In Flask APIs, this can include testing interactions with databases, external services, and other dependencies.

Key Characteristics:

- Focuses on the integration of multiple components.
- Tests the API in a more realistic environment, often involving actual database connections or service calls.
- Typically slower than unit tests but essential for ensuring that components interact correctly.

CHAPTER 7: TESTING FLASK APIS: STRATEGIES AND BEST PRACTICES

Example of Integration Testing: You can extend the previous example to include integration testing by setting up a test database:

```python
Copy code
@pytest.fixture
def test_client():
    app.config['TESTING'] = True
    app.config['SQLALCHEMY_DATABASE_URI'] = 'sqlite:///:memory:'
    # Use an in-memory database for testing
    with app.test_client() as client:
        with app.app_context():
            # Create the database and tables
            db.create_all()
            yield client
            db.drop_all()  # Cleanup after tests

def test_create_user(test_client):
    response = test_client.post('/api/users', json={"username": "testuser"})
    assert response.status_code == 201
    assert b"User created" in response.data
```

In this example, we create a temporary in-memory SQLite database for testing, ensuring that tests do not affect the production database.

C. End-to-End Testing

End-to-end (E2E) testing involves testing the entire application flow, from the front-end to the back-end. E2E tests simulate user interactions and verify that the application behaves as expected.

Key Characteristics:

- Tests the complete flow of the application, including user interactions and data retrieval.
- Often uses tools like Selenium or Cypress to automate browser interactions.
- Typically slower than unit and integration tests due to the complexity of the tests.

Example of E2E Testing with Cypress: To set up end-to-end testing with Cypress, follow these steps:

1. **Install Cypress**:

```bash
Copy code
npm install cypress --save-dev
```

1. **Create a Cypress Test File** (e.g., cypress/integration/api_spec.js):

```javascript
Copy code
describe('Flask API E2E Tests', () => {
    it('should load the home page', () => {
        cy.visit('http://localhost:5000/');
        cy.contains('Welcome to your first serverless Flask
        API!');
    });

    it('should retrieve data from the API', () => {
        cy.request('GET', 'http://localhost:5000/api/data')
            .its('body')
            .should('deep.equal', { data: 'This is some data!' });
    });
});
```

In this example, Cypress tests verify that the home page loads correctly and that the API retrieves data as expected.

3. Tools for Testing Flask APIs

Several tools and frameworks can facilitate testing in Flask applications:

A. Testing Frameworks

1. **unittest**: The built-in Python testing framework, suitable for writing unit tests.
2. **pytest**: A powerful testing framework that simplifies the process of writing tests and offers advanced features like fixtures and plugins.

B. Mocking Libraries

When testing APIs that interact with external services, it's essential to use mocking to simulate those interactions:

1. **unittest.mock**: A built-in Python library for creating mock objects to replace external services during testing.
2. **responses**: A library for mocking HTTP responses, useful when testing APIs that make external HTTP requests.

Example of Using unittest.mock:

```python
Copy code
from unittest.mock import patch

@patch('app.requests.get')  # Mocking the requests.get method
def test_external_api_call(client, mock_get):
    mock_get.return_value.json.return_value = {"data": "Mocked data"}
    response = client.get('/api/external-data')
    assert response.status_code == 200
    assert response.json == {"data": "Mocked data"}
```

In this example, we use unittest.mock to replace the requests.get method with a mock object, allowing us to simulate external API calls without making actual requests.

C. Continuous Integration Tools

Integrating testing into your CI/CD pipeline is essential for ensuring that changes to the codebase do not introduce new bugs. Popular CI/CD tools include:

1. **GitHub Actions**: A flexible CI/CD tool integrated with GitHub, allowing you to define workflows to run tests automatically on code changes.
2. **Travis CI**: A cloud-based CI service that automatically builds and tests your code based on your repository's settings.

Example of a GitHub Actions Workflow:
Create a .github/workflows/test.yml file in your repository:

```yaml
Copy code
name: CI

on: [push, pull_request]

jobs:
  test:
    runs-on: ubuntu-latest

    services:
      db:
        image: postgres:latest
        ports:
          - 5432:5432
        env:
          POSTGRES_USER: user
          POSTGRES_PASSWORD: password
          POSTGRES_DB: test_db
        options: >-
          --health-cmd "pg_isready -U user" --health-interval 10s
          --health-timeout 5s --health-retries 5

    steps:
    - uses: actions/checkout@v2
    - name: Set up Python
      uses: actions/setup-python@v2
      with:
        python-version: '3.8'
```

```
- name: Install dependencies
  run: |
    pip install -r requirements.txt
    pip install pytest
- name: Run tests
  run: |
    pytest tests/
```

This workflow installs dependencies and runs tests whenever code is pushed or a pull request is created.

4. Best Practices for Testing Flask APIs

Implementing effective testing strategies involves following best practices to ensure your tests are reliable, maintainable, and comprehensive.

A. Write Clear and Descriptive Tests

1. **Naming Conventions**: Use clear and descriptive names for your test functions to convey their purpose. For example, use test_user_creation_success instead of a generic name like test_function1.
2. **Document Test Cases**: Include comments or docstrings to describe the expected behavior of the tests, making it easier for others (or your future self) to understand the purpose of each test.

B. Keep Tests Isolated

1. **Avoid Side Effects**: Ensure that tests do not depend on the outcome of other tests. Each test should be independent and capable of running in isolation.
2. **Use Fixtures**: Utilize testing frameworks' fixture capabilities to set up test data and environments, ensuring that each test starts with a clean slate.

C. Run Tests Frequently

1. **Automate Testing**: Set up automated testing in your CI/CD pipeline

to run tests on every code change. This helps catch issues early in the development process.
2. **Run Tests Locally**: Encourage developers to run tests locally before pushing changes to the repository. This practice reduces the likelihood of introducing bugs into the codebase.

D. Prioritize Critical Paths

Focus on testing the most critical paths and features of your API first. Prioritize tests for key endpoints and functionality to ensure that your application remains stable as it evolves.

E. Implement Performance Testing

In addition to functional testing, consider implementing performance tests to evaluate how your Flask API performs under load. Use tools like **Apache JMeter**, **Locust**, or **Gatling** to simulate user traffic and assess performance metrics.

5. Example Testing Scenarios

To further illustrate the testing concepts covered in this chapter, we will explore example testing scenarios for a hypothetical Flask API that provides user management functionality.

A. Scenario 1: User Registration

Objective: Test the user registration endpoint to ensure it handles valid and invalid inputs correctly.

Test Cases:

1. **Successful Registration**: Test that a valid request returns a 201 status code and a success message.
2. **Duplicate Username**: Test that a registration attempt with an existing username returns a 409 status code and an appropriate error message.
3. **Missing Fields**: Test that a request missing required fields returns a 400 status code and an error message.

Example Test Implementation:

```python
Copy code
def test_user_registration(client):
    # Test successful registration
    response = client.post('/api/register', json={"username":
    "newuser", "password": "password123"})
    assert response.status_code == 201
    assert b"User registered successfully" in response.data

    # Test duplicate username
    response = client.post('/api/register', json={"username":
    "newuser", "password": "password123"})
    assert response.status_code == 409
    assert b"Username already exists" in response.data

    # Test missing fields
    response = client.post('/api/register', json={"username":
    "anotheruser"})
    assert response.status_code == 400
    assert b"Missing required fields" in response.data
```

B. Scenario 2: User Authentication

Objective: Test the user authentication endpoint to ensure it properly authenticates users.

Test Cases:

1. **Successful Authentication**: Test that a valid username and password return a 200 status code and a JWT token.
2. **Invalid Credentials**: Test that an authentication attempt with incorrect credentials returns a 401 status code and an error message.

Example Test Implementation:

```python
Copy code
def test_user_authentication(client):
    # Assuming the user "newuser" was registered in the previous
```

```
test
response = client.post('/api/auth/login', json={"username":
"newuser", "password": "password123"})
assert response.status_code == 200
assert 'token' in response.json

# Test invalid credentials
response = client.post('/api/auth/login', json={"username":
"newuser", "password": "wrongpassword"})
assert response.status_code == 401
assert b"Invalid credentials" in response.data
```

Conclusion

In this chapter, we explored the critical role of testing in Flask API development, emphasizing the importance of ensuring that APIs function correctly, are secure, and provide a positive user experience. We discussed various types of testing, including unit testing, integration testing, and end-to-end testing, along with the tools and frameworks available to facilitate testing in Flask applications.

We also covered best practices for effective testing, such as writing clear and descriptive tests, keeping tests isolated, and implementing performance testing. Through example testing scenarios, we illustrated how to apply these concepts in real-world applications.

Chapter 8: Deploying Flask APIs to Production

Deploying a Flask API to production is a critical step in the software development lifecycle. A successful deployment ensures that your application is accessible to users, performs reliably under load, and is secure from vulnerabilities. In this chapter, we will explore various strategies for deploying Flask APIs, focusing on the deployment process, infrastructure options, continuous integration/continuous deployment (CI/CD) practices, monitoring, and best practices for maintaining a production-ready API.

1. Understanding the Deployment Process

Deploying a Flask API involves several key steps, from preparing the application for deployment to configuring the production environment. Understanding this process is essential for ensuring a smooth deployment.

A. Preparing Your Flask Application

Before deploying your Flask API, you should prepare your application to ensure it runs smoothly in a production environment.

1. **Environment Configuration**: Set up separate configuration files for development and production. Use environment variables to manage sensitive information, such as database credentials and API keys.
2. **Example**:

```python
Copy code
import os

class Config:
    SQLALCHEMY_DATABASE_URI = os.environ.get('DATABASE_URL')
    SECRET_KEY = os.environ.get('SECRET_KEY')
```

1. **Dependency Management**: Use a requirements.txt file to specify

your application's dependencies. This file allows you to recreate the environment easily on the production server.
2. **Example**:

```bash
Copy code
pip freeze > requirements.txt
```

1. **Static Files**: If your application serves static files (e.g., images, CSS, JavaScript), ensure that these files are properly organized and accessible.
2. **Testing**: Thoroughly test your application in a staging environment that closely mirrors production. Ensure that all functionality works as expected before deploying to production.

B. Choosing a Deployment Environment

The choice of deployment environment significantly affects the performance, scalability, and maintenance of your Flask API. Common deployment options include:

1. **Platform as a Service (PaaS)**: Services like Heroku, Google App Engine, and AWS Elastic Beanstalk provide a simplified deployment experience, allowing you to focus on your application rather than infrastructure management.
2. **Containerization**: Using Docker to containerize your Flask application enables you to create lightweight, portable containers that can be deployed consistently across different environments.
3. **Serverless Architecture**: Deploying your Flask API as a serverless application using AWS Lambda or Azure Functions allows you to automatically scale based on demand, minimizing operational overhead.
4. **Virtual Private Server (VPS)**: Deploying on a VPS (e.g., DigitalOcean, Linode) gives you more control over the server environment but

requires you to manage server configuration, scaling, and security.

2. Deployment Steps for Flask APIs

Deploying a Flask API involves several key steps, regardless of the deployment environment you choose.

A. Setting Up the Production Environment

1. **Provision the Server**: If deploying to a VPS, provision your server with the required specifications (CPU, memory, storage) based on your expected traffic.
2. **Install Dependencies**: Install the necessary software on the server, including Python, a web server (e.g., Nginx or Apache), and any required libraries.
3. **Clone Your Repository**: Clone your application code from your version control system (e.g., GitHub, GitLab) to the production server.

```bash
Copy code
git clone https://github.com/username/repo.git
```

1. **Set Up a Virtual Environment**: Create a virtual environment for your Flask application to manage dependencies separately from the system Python installation.

```bash
Copy code
cd repo
python3 -m venv venv
source venv/bin/activate
```

1. **Install Application Dependencies**:

```bash
Copy code
pip install -r requirements.txt
```

B. Configuring the Web Server

A web server acts as a reverse proxy, forwarding requests to your Flask application. Common choices include Nginx and Apache.

1. **Nginx Configuration Example**:
2. Create a new configuration file for your Flask application:

```nginx
Copy code
server {
    listen 80;
    server_name your_domain.com;

    location / {
        proxy_pass http://127.0.0.1:5000;  # Flask app runs on port 5000
        proxy_set_header Host $host;
        proxy_set_header X-Real-IP $remote_addr;
        proxy_set_header X-Forwarded-For $proxy_add_x_forwarded_for;
        proxy_set_header X-Forwarded-Proto $scheme;
    }
}
```

1. **Starting the Flask Application**: Use a WSGI server such as Gunicorn or uWSGI to run your Flask application in production.
2. **Example with Gunicorn**:

```bash
Copy code
gunicorn --bind 127.0.0.1:5000 wsgi:app  # Replace wsgi:app with
your app's entry point
```

1. **Testing the Configuration**: Restart the web server and test the configuration to ensure it forwards requests correctly.

```bash
Copy code
sudo nginx -t
sudo systemctl restart nginx
```

3. Continuous Integration/Continuous Deployment (CI/CD)

Implementing CI/CD practices streamlines the deployment process, allowing for faster and more reliable updates to your Flask API.

A. Setting Up a CI/CD Pipeline

1. **Version Control**: Ensure that your code is hosted in a version control system (e.g., Git). This provides a history of changes and allows for collaboration.
2. **Automated Testing**: Integrate automated testing into your CI/CD pipeline to ensure that code changes do not introduce new bugs. Use tools like pytest or unittest to run tests automatically on code changes.
3. **Build and Deploy Steps**: Define the steps for building and deploying your application in your CI/CD configuration. For example, you might use GitHub Actions, Travis CI, or CircleCI.

Example GitHub Actions Workflow:

CHAPTER 8: DEPLOYING FLASK APIS TO PRODUCTION

```yaml
Copy code
name: CI/CD Pipeline

on:
  push:
    branches: [ main ]
  pull_request:
    branches: [ main ]

jobs:
  build:
    runs-on: ubuntu-latest

    steps:
      - uses: actions/checkout@v2
      - name: Set up Python
        uses: actions/setup-python@v2
        with:
          python-version: '3.8'
      - name: Install dependencies
        run: |
          pip install -r requirements.txt
          pip install pytest
      - name: Run tests
        run: |
          pytest tests/
      - name: Deploy to Server
        run: |
          ssh user@your_server "cd /path/to/your/app && git pull && source venv/bin/activate && pip install -r requirements.txt && sudo systemctl restart nginx"
```

In this example, the workflow checks out the code, sets up the Python environment, installs dependencies, runs tests, and deploys the application to the server.

4. Monitoring and Logging

Once your Flask API is deployed, monitoring its performance and logging important events is crucial for maintaining reliability.

A. Monitoring API Performance

1. **Use AWS CloudWatch**: If your API is deployed on AWS Lambda, you can leverage CloudWatch to monitor performance metrics, such as invocation counts, error rates, and latency.
2. **Application Performance Monitoring (APM)**: Consider using APM tools like New Relic, Datadog, or Sentry to monitor the performance of your application in real-time, identify bottlenecks, and gain insights into user behavior.

B. Logging Events

1. **Structured Logging**: Implement structured logging in your Flask application to capture relevant information about requests and errors. Use Python's built-in logging module to configure logging.
2. **Example**:

```python
Copy code
import logging

logging.basicConfig(level=logging.INFO)

@app.route('/api/data')
def get_data():
    app.logger.info('Fetching data...')
    return jsonify({"data": "This is some data!"})
```

1. **Log Aggregation**: Use log aggregation tools such as ELK Stack (Elasticsearch, Logstash, Kibana) or Splunk to collect and analyze logs from your application, helping you identify issues and trends.

5. Handling Updates and Maintenance

Maintaining a production-ready API requires ongoing effort to ensure that it continues to perform well and meets user needs.

A. Managing Application Updates

1. **Staging Environment**: Set up a staging environment that mirrors your production environment. Use this environment to test updates and new features before deploying them to production.
2. **Rolling Deployments**: Consider implementing rolling deployments to gradually roll out changes to your application. This approach reduces the risk of downtime or failures affecting all users at once.
3. **Backup Strategies**: Regularly back up your database and application data to prevent data loss. Automate backups using scripts or cloud services.

B. Security Updates

1. **Regularly Update Dependencies**: Keep your application dependencies up to date to ensure that you benefit from the latest security patches and features. Use tools like pip-audit to identify vulnerable packages.
2. **Monitor Security Vulnerabilities**: Use vulnerability scanning tools like Snyk or OWASP Dependency-Check to monitor your application for known security vulnerabilities.

6. Best Practices for Deploying Flask APIs

To ensure a successful deployment and smooth operation of your Flask APIs, follow these best practices:

A. Follow Twelve-Factor App Principles

The Twelve-Factor App methodology outlines best practices for building modern web applications. Key principles include:

1. **Codebase**: Maintain a single codebase for your application, tracked in version control.
2. **Dependencies**: Explicitly declare and isolate dependencies using a

package manager.
3. **Configuration**: Store configuration in the environment, separating it from code.
4. **Backing Services**: Treat backing services (databases, queues) as attached resources.
5. **Build, Release, Run**: Strictly separate the build and run stages of the application.

B. Use HTTPS

Always deploy your API over HTTPS to ensure secure communication between clients and the server. Use SSL/TLS certificates from trusted certificate authorities.

C. Implement Rate Limiting

To prevent abuse and ensure fair usage of your API, implement rate limiting on your endpoints. Use API Gateway or middleware to enforce limits.

D. Document Your API

Provide comprehensive documentation for your API, including endpoints, request/response formats, authentication methods, and usage examples. Use tools like Swagger or Postman to generate and maintain API documentation.

E. Plan for Scaling

As your application grows, be prepared to scale your infrastructure. Consider using auto-scaling groups, load balancers, and caching strategies to handle increased traffic.

Conclusion

In this chapter, we covered the essential steps and strategies for deploying Flask APIs to production. We began by understanding the deployment process, emphasizing the importance of preparing your application and choosing the right deployment environment.

We explored the deployment steps, including setting up the production environment, configuring the web server, and implementing CI/CD practices to streamline the deployment process. Monitoring and logging were discussed as crucial components for maintaining the health and performance

CHAPTER 8: DEPLOYING FLASK APIS TO PRODUCTION

of your API in production.

We also addressed the importance of handling updates and maintenance, as well as best practices for deploying Flask APIs. By following these guidelines, you can ensure a successful deployment and maintain a reliable, secure, and high-performing API.

Chapter 8: Advanced Topics in Flask Development

Flask is a powerful micro web framework that allows developers to build web applications quickly and flexibly. While you may have already learned the foundational concepts of Flask development, this chapter will delve into advanced topics that can enhance your applications and provide a more robust user experience. We will cover implementing WebSockets for real-time communication, creating background tasks with Celery, optimizing database interactions, utilizing Flask extensions for added functionality, and securing your application against common vulnerabilities.

1. Implementing WebSockets in Flask

WebSockets enable real-time, bidirectional communication between clients and servers, making them ideal for applications like chat services, live notifications, and real-time updates. Flask can handle WebSockets using libraries like Flask-SocketIO, which simplifies the integration of WebSockets into your Flask applications.

    A. Setting Up Flask-SocketIO

      1. **Installation**: To use Flask-SocketIO, you need to install the package along with its dependencies.

CHAPTER 8: ADVANCED TOPICS IN FLASK DEVELOPMENT

```bash
Copy code
pip install flask-socketio
```

1. **Basic Usage**: Here's a basic example of how to set up Flask-SocketIO in your application:

```python
Copy code
from flask import Flask, render_template
from flask_socketio import SocketIO

app = Flask(__name__)
socketio = SocketIO(app)

@app.route('/')
def index():
    return render_template('index.html')

@socketio.on('message')
def handle_message(msg):
    print('Received message: ' + msg)
    socketio.send('Message received: ' + msg)

if __name__ == '__main__':
    socketio.run(app)
```

In this example, we create a basic Flask application that listens for messages from clients and sends a response back. The @socketio.on('message') decorator defines an event handler for incoming messages.

1. **Client-Side Implementation**: To interact with the server, you'll need to add client-side JavaScript code to your HTML template to establish a WebSocket connection.

2. Example index.html:

```
html
Copy code
<!DOCTYPE html>
<html>
<head>
    <title>WebSocket Example</title>
    <script
    src="https://cdn.socket.io/4.0.0/socket.io.min.js"></script>
    <script>
        const socket = io();

        socket.on('connect', () => {
            console.log('Connected to WebSocket server.');
        });

        function sendMessage() {
            const message =
            document.getElementById('messageInput').value;
            socket.send(message);
        }

        socket.on('message', (msg) => {
            const messages = document.getElementById('messages');
            messages.innerHTML += '<li>' + msg + '</li>';
        });
    </script>
</head>
<body>
    <h1>WebSocket Example</h1>
    <input id="messageInput" type="text" placeholder="Type a
    message">
    <button onclick="sendMessage()">Send</button>
    <ul id="messages"></ul>
</body>
</html>
```

In this HTML template, we use the Socket.IO client library to establish a

CHAPTER 8: ADVANCED TOPICS IN FLASK DEVELOPMENT

connection to the server, send messages, and display incoming messages in a list.

B. Handling Events and Broadcasting

Flask-SocketIO allows you to handle various events and broadcast messages to multiple clients. This capability is essential for building applications like chat rooms or collaborative editing tools.

1. **Broadcasting Messages**: You can broadcast messages to all connected clients using the emit method.

```python
Copy code
@socketio.on('message')
def handle_message(msg):
    print('Received message: ' + msg)
    socketio.send('Message received: ' + msg, broadcast=True)
```

1. **Custom Events**: You can define custom events for specific actions within your application.

```python
Copy code
@socketio.on('join')
def handle_join(username):
    print(f'{username} has joined the chat.')
    socketio.emit('message', f'{username} has joined the chat.', broadcast=True)
```

1. **Namespaces**: Flask-SocketIO supports namespaces, allowing you to segment WebSocket connections based on specific routes or functionality.

```python
Copy code
@socketio.on('connect', namespace='/chat')
def handle_connect():
    print('Client connected to chat namespace.')
```

2. Creating Background Tasks with Celery

In web applications, certain tasks can be time-consuming, such as sending emails, processing files, or making external API calls. Offloading these tasks to background workers helps keep your API responsive. Celery is a distributed task queue that makes it easy to handle background tasks in Flask applications.

A. Setting Up Celery

1. **Installation**: Install Celery along with a message broker like Redis or RabbitMQ.

```bash
Copy code
pip install celery[redis]
```

1. **Basic Configuration**: Here's how to configure Celery with Flask:

```python
Copy code
from flask import Flask
from celery import Celery

app = Flask(__name__)
```

```
app.config['CELERY_BROKER_URL'] = 'redis://localhost:6379/0'  #
Set up Redis as the broker
app.config['CELERY_RESULT_BACKEND'] = 'redis://localhost:6379/0'

celery = Celery(app.name, broker=app.config['CELERY_BROKER_URL'])
celery.conf.update(app.config)

@celery.task
def long_running_task(data):
    import time
    time.sleep(10)   # Simulate a long task
    return f"Processed {data}"
```

In this example, we set up Celery to use Redis as the message broker and define a long-running task.

1. **Creating Background Tasks**: You can create tasks that run in the background, allowing your API to respond quickly.

```python
Copy code
@app.route('/api/start-task/<data>', methods=['POST'])
def start_task(data):
    task = long_running_task.apply_async(args=[data])
    return jsonify({"task_id": task.id}), 202
```

In this endpoint, we start a background task and return a task ID to the client.

B. Monitoring Task Status

Celery provides the ability to monitor the status of tasks and retrieve their results.

1. **Checking Task Status**:

```python
Copy code
from celery.result import AsyncResult

@app.route('/api/task-status/<task_id>', methods=['GET'])
def task_status(task_id):
    task_result = AsyncResult(task_id)
    return jsonify({"task_id": task_id, "status":
    task_result.status}), 200
```

This endpoint allows clients to check the status of a task by its ID.

1. **Result Backend**: If you want to return results to the client, ensure you have configured a result backend in Celery (e.g., Redis, RabbitMQ, or a database).

3. Optimizing Database Interactions

Flask applications often interact with databases, and optimizing these interactions is crucial for performance. Here are some strategies to improve database efficiency:

A. Use Connection Pooling

Connection pooling allows your application to reuse database connections rather than creating new ones for each request. Flask-SQLAlchemy supports connection pooling out of the box.

1. **Configure Connection Pooling**:

```python
Copy code
app.config['SQLALCHEMY_DATABASE_URI'] =
'mysql+pymysql://user:password@localhost/dbname'
app.config['SQLALCHEMY_ENGINE_OPTIONS'] = {
    'pool_size': 10,
```

```
    'max_overflow': 20,
    'pool_timeout': 30,
}
```

This configuration sets up a connection pool with a maximum of 10 connections.

B. Optimize Query Performance

1. **Indexing**: Use database indexing to speed up query performance. Identify columns frequently used in WHERE clauses or JOINs and create indexes accordingly.
2. **Batch Queries**: Instead of making multiple queries, batch them together to reduce the number of round trips to the database.
3. **Use Eager Loading**: If your application frequently accesses related data, consider using eager loading to minimize the number of queries made.

```python
Copy code
users = User.query.options(joinedload(User.profile)).all()
```

This query retrieves all users along with their associated profiles in a single query.

C. Caching Database Queries

Implement caching for frequently accessed data to reduce load on the database.

1. **Use Flask-Caching**: Integrate Flask-Caching to cache database query results.

```python
Copy code
from flask_caching import Cache

cache = Cache(app, config={'CACHE_TYPE': 'simple'})

@cache.cached(timeout=300, query_string=True)
@app.route('/api/users')
def get_users():
    users = User.query.all()
    return jsonify([user.to_dict() for user in users])
```

In this example, the result of the /api/users endpoint is cached for 5 minutes.

4. Utilizing Flask Extensions

Flask extensions provide additional functionality that can simplify development and enhance your applications. Here are some commonly used Flask extensions:

A. Flask-RESTful

Flask-RESTful is an extension that simplifies building RESTful APIs with Flask. It provides tools for creating resources, parsing request data, and generating responses.

1. **Installation**:

```bash
Copy code
pip install flask-restful
```

1. **Creating Resources**:

CHAPTER 8: ADVANCED TOPICS IN FLASK DEVELOPMENT

```python
Copy code
from flask_restful import Api, Resource

api = Api(app)

class UserResource(Resource):
    def get(self, user_id):
        user = User.query.get(user_id)
        return user.to_dict() if user else {'message': 'User not found'}, 404

api.add_resource(UserResource, '/api/users/<int:user_id>')
```

In this example, we create a RESTful resource for managing user data.

B. Flask-Migrate

Flask-Migrate is an extension that handles SQLAlchemy database migrations, allowing you to manage changes to your database schema.

1. **Installation**:

```bash
Copy code
pip install flask-migrate
```

1. **Setting Up Migrations**:

```python
Copy code
from flask_migrate import Migrate

migrate = Migrate(app, db)
```

```
# Initialize migration repository
flask db init
```

1. **Creating and Applying Migrations**:

```
bash
Copy code
flask db migrate -m "Initial migration"
flask db upgrade
```

These commands create a migration script and apply the changes to your database.

5. Securing Your Flask Application

Security is a critical aspect of any web application. When deploying a Flask API, it's essential to implement security measures to protect against common vulnerabilities.

A. Protecting Against Common Vulnerabilities

1. **Cross-Site Scripting (XSS)**: Sanitize user inputs to prevent malicious scripts from being injected. Use libraries like bleach to clean input data.

```
bash
Copy code
pip install bleach
python
Copy code
from bleach import clean

@app.route('/api/submit', methods=['POST'])
def submit_data():
    data = request.json.get('data')
```

CHAPTER 8: ADVANCED TOPICS IN FLASK DEVELOPMENT

```
sanitized_data = clean(data)
# Process sanitized data
```

1. **SQL Injection**: Use parameterized queries to protect against SQL injection attacks.

```python
Copy code
user = User.query.filter_by(username=username).first()  # Safe from injection
```

1. **Cross-Site Request Forgery (CSRF)**: Protect your application from CSRF attacks by using CSRF tokens.

```bash
Copy code
pip install flask-wtf
```
```python
Copy code
from flask_wtf.csrf import CSRFProtect

csrf = CSRFProtect(app)
```

B. Securing API Endpoints

1. **Authentication**: Implement authentication mechanisms such as OAuth2, JWT, or API keys to secure your API endpoints.
2. **Authorization**: Ensure that users have appropriate permissions to access specific resources. Use role-based access control (RBAC) to manage user roles.
3. **Rate Limiting**: Implement rate limiting to prevent abuse and protect

your API from excessive requests.

```bash
Copy code
pip install flask-limiter
```
```python
Copy code
from flask_limiter import Limiter

limiter = Limiter(app, key_func=get_remote_address)

@limiter.limit("5 per minute")  # Limit to 5 requests per minute
@app.route('/api/data')
def get_data():
    return jsonify({"data": "This is some data!"})
```

6. Conclusion

In this chapter, we explored advanced topics in Flask development, focusing on enhancing your applications through the implementation of WebSockets, background tasks with Celery, database optimization, the use of Flask extensions, and securing your applications against common vulnerabilities.

We started by discussing the power of WebSockets for real-time communication, demonstrating how to set up Flask-SocketIO to handle bi-directional messaging. Next, we covered the importance of background task management using Celery, allowing you to offload long-running tasks to keep your API responsive.

Optimizing database interactions was another key topic, where we emphasized the importance of connection pooling, query optimization, and caching to improve performance. We also highlighted various Flask extensions that simplify common tasks, such as Flask-RESTful for building RESTful APIs and Flask-Migrate for managing database migrations.

Finally, we focused on security best practices to protect your Flask applications, including protecting against XSS, SQL injection, and CSRF attacks, as well as implementing authentication, authorization, and rate limiting.

Chapter 9: API Documentation: Best Practices and Tools

Creating comprehensive and user-friendly API documentation is essential for ensuring that developers can effectively understand, integrate, and utilize your API. Good documentation enhances the user experience, reduces support requests, and can ultimately lead to greater adoption of your API. This chapter will explore the principles of effective API documentation, the various tools available to create and maintain documentation, and best practices for structuring and presenting your API information.

1. The Importance of API Documentation

API documentation serves as the primary source of information for developers who want to integrate with your API. It provides details on how to use the API, including endpoints, request/response formats, authentication methods, and error handling.

   A. Key Benefits of API Documentation
   1. **Ease of Integration**: Clear documentation allows developers to quickly understand how to integrate with your API, reducing the time it takes to build applications.
   2. **Reduced Support Load**: Well-documented APIs minimize the need for external support by providing answers to common questions and

CHAPTER 9: API DOCUMENTATION: BEST PRACTICES AND TOOLS

issues, enabling developers to resolve problems independently.
3. **Improved User Experience**: High-quality documentation enhances the overall user experience, making it easier for developers to work with your API and increasing satisfaction.
4. **Increased Adoption**: APIs with clear, concise documentation are more likely to attract developers, leading to higher adoption rates.
5. **Facilitates Maintenance**: Proper documentation helps ensure that updates and changes to the API are communicated effectively, maintaining developer trust and usability.

2. Principles of Effective API Documentation

To create effective API documentation, adhere to the following principles:

A. Clarity and Simplicity

1. **Use Plain Language**: Write documentation in clear, straightforward language that is easy to understand, avoiding technical jargon where possible.
2. **Be Consistent**: Use consistent terminology and formatting throughout your documentation to avoid confusion. Define any specific terms used in your API.
3. **Structure Information Logically**: Organize documentation logically, grouping related information together and using clear headings and subheadings.

B. Comprehensive Coverage

1. **Detailed Endpoint Descriptions**: Provide thorough descriptions of each API endpoint, including the method (GET, POST, etc.), URL, parameters, request body, and expected responses.
2. **Authentication Methods**: Clearly explain how to authenticate with the API, detailing any required tokens, API keys, or OAuth flows.
3. **Error Handling**: Document possible error responses, including status codes, error messages, and suggested resolutions.

C. Visual Aids

1. **Use Code Samples**: Include code snippets to demonstrate how to use the API. These examples should cover various programming languages and libraries when possible.
2. **Flowcharts and Diagrams**: Visual aids can help clarify complex processes, such as authentication flows or data interactions.
3. **Swagger/OpenAPI Documentation**: Utilize tools that generate visual documentation based on API specifications, allowing developers to explore the API interactively.

3. Tools for API Documentation

Several tools are available to help you create, manage, and publish API documentation. Below are some popular options:

A. Swagger/OpenAPI

Overview: Swagger is a framework for API documentation that utilizes the OpenAPI Specification (OAS) to describe RESTful APIs. It provides a user-friendly interface for developers to explore APIs interactively.

Key Features:

- Generate interactive API documentation that developers can use to test endpoints.
- Support for various programming languages and frameworks.
- Ability to define request/response formats, authentication methods, and error codes.

Example: To use Swagger with a Flask application, you can use the flasgger extension:

1. **Installation**:

CHAPTER 9: API DOCUMENTATION: BEST PRACTICES AND TOOLS

```bash
Copy code
pip install flasgger
```

1. **Example Setup**:

```python
Copy code
from flask import Flask
from flasgger import Swagger

app = Flask(__name__)
swagger = Swagger(app)

@app.route('/api/users', methods=['GET'])
def get_users():
    """
    Retrieve a list of users.
    ---
    responses:
      200:
        description: A list of users
        schema:
          type: array
          items:
            type: object
            properties:
              id:
                type: integer
                example: 1
              username:
                type: string
                example: testuser
    """
    users = [{"id": 1, "username": "testuser"}]
    return jsonify(users), 200
```

```
if __name__ == '__main__':
    app.run(debug=True)
```

In this example, we use flasgger to define the API documentation directly in the endpoint function using docstrings.

B. Postman

Overview: Postman is a popular tool for API development that also offers capabilities for documenting APIs. It allows you to create collections of requests and provides an interface for testing and sharing APIs.

Key Features:

- Create documentation directly from Postman collections.
- Share collections and documentation with team members or the public.
- Generate code snippets for different programming languages.

Example:

1. Create a collection of requests in Postman.
2. Use the documentation feature to add descriptions, examples, and notes for each request.
3. Publish the documentation for easy access.

C. Read the Docs

Overview: Read the Docs is a platform that hosts documentation for open-source projects. It supports Markdown and reStructuredText formats, making it easy to write and publish documentation.

Key Features:

- Automatic builds of documentation from your repository.
- Versioning support to maintain documentation for different API versions.
- Search functionality for easy navigation.

Example:

1. Write your documentation in Markdown or reStructuredText format.
2. Configure Read the Docs to build your documentation from your version control system (e.g., GitHub).
3. Publish and share the documentation with users.
4. Structuring Your API Documentation

Structuring your API documentation effectively is crucial for usability. Below is a recommended structure for organizing your documentation:

A. Overview

- **Introduction**: Provide a brief overview of your API, its purpose, and the problems it solves.
- **Getting Started**: Include instructions for obtaining access to the API (e.g., signing up for an API key) and an overview of the authentication process.

B. Authentication

- **Authentication Methods**: Detail the authentication methods supported by your API (e.g., API keys, OAuth2).
- **Example Authentication Flow**: Provide examples of how to authenticate and include sample requests.

C. API Endpoints

- **Endpoint Structure**: For each endpoint, include the following sections:
- **Endpoint URL**: The URL for the endpoint.
- **HTTP Method**: The HTTP method used (GET, POST, etc.).
- **Parameters**: Describe any query parameters or path parameters required for the request.
- **Request Body**: Provide details on the request body, including required

and optional fields.
- **Response Format**: Document the expected response format, including success and error responses.
- **Examples**: Include code snippets demonstrating how to interact with the endpoint.

D. Error Handling

- **Error Codes**: List all possible error codes and their meanings.
- **Error Responses**: Provide examples of error responses, including sample messages.

E. Rate Limiting and Quotas

- **Usage Limits**: Explain any rate limits or quotas imposed on the API and how users can monitor their usage.
- **Handling Rate Limit Errors**: Provide guidance on how to handle rate limit errors when they occur.

F. Additional Resources

- **SDKs and Libraries**: If available, provide links to SDKs or libraries that simplify integration with your API.
- **Support and Contact Information**: Include information on how users can reach out for support or report issues.

5. Writing API Documentation

Writing effective API documentation involves a clear, concise, and consistent approach. Here are some tips for writing high-quality documentation:

A. Use Simple Language

1. **Avoid Jargon**: Use language that is easily understandable by developers of varying expertise levels. Avoid technical jargon unless necessary,

and define any specialized terms.
2. **Be Direct**: Use a straightforward writing style that conveys information clearly. Avoid unnecessary fluff or overly complex sentences.

B. Provide Clear Examples

1. **Code Samples**: Include code samples that demonstrate how to use the API effectively. Use a variety of programming languages to cater to a broader audience.
2. **Request/Response Examples**: Provide examples of actual requests and responses for each endpoint, including both successful and error scenarios.

C. Keep Documentation Up to Date

1. **Version Control**: Maintain documentation versions to reflect changes in the API. Ensure that users can access the documentation for the specific version of the API they are using.
2. **Regular Reviews**: Schedule regular reviews of your documentation to ensure it remains accurate and up to date. Encourage team members to report discrepancies or suggest improvements.

6. Example of Comprehensive API Documentation

Below is a structured example of API documentation for a fictional user management API:

User Management API Documentation

Overview

The User Management API provides endpoints for managing user accounts, including registration, authentication, and profile management.

Getting Started

To use the User Management API, sign up for an API key at [yourwebsite.com/signup]. Once you have your API key, include it in the Authorization header for all requests.

Authentication

The User Management API uses API key-based authentication. Include your API key in the header of each request.
Example:

```http
Copy code
Authorization: Bearer your_api_key_here
```

API Endpoints

1. User Registration

- **Endpoint URL**: /api/users/register
- **HTTP Method**: POST
- **Request Body**:
- username (string, required): The username for the new user.
- password (string, required): The password for the new user.

Example Request:

```json
Copy code
{
  "username": "newuser",
```

CHAPTER 9: API DOCUMENTATION: BEST PRACTICES AND TOOLS

```
  "password": "password123"
}
```

Response:

- **201 Created**: User registered successfully.
- **409 Conflict**: Username already exists.

Example Response:

```json
Copy code
{
  "message": "User registered successfully."
}
```

2. User Authentication

- **Endpoint URL**: /api/users/login
- **HTTP Method**: POST
- **Request Body**:
- username (string, required): The username of the user.
- password (string, required): The password of the user.

Example Request:

```json
Copy code
{
  "username": "newuser",
  "password": "password123"
}
```

Response:

- **200 OK**: Authentication successful, returns a JWT token.
- **401 Unauthorized**: Invalid credentials.

Example Response:

```json
Copy code
{
  "token": "your_jwt_token_here"
}
```

Error Handling

Status CodeDescription
  400
  Bad Request: Invalid input data
  401
  Unauthorized: Invalid credentials
  409
  Conflict: Resource already exists
  500
  Internal Server Error: Unexpected error

Rate Limiting

The User Management API enforces rate limiting to prevent abuse. Users are limited to 100 requests per hour. Exceeding this limit will result in a 429 Too Many Requests response.

Example Error Response:

```json
Copy code
```

CHAPTER 9: API DOCUMENTATION: BEST PRACTICES AND TOOLS

```
{
  "error": "Too Many Requests",
  "message": "You have exceeded the rate limit."
}
```

Support

For support, please contact our support team at support@yourwebsite.com or visit our support page.

Conclusion

In this chapter, we explored the importance of API documentation and the principles of creating effective documentation. We discussed various tools, including Swagger/OpenAPI, Postman, and Read the Docs, to help you generate and maintain documentation for your APIs. We also covered best practices for structuring your documentation, writing clearly, and keeping it up to date.

High-quality API documentation is crucial for enhancing the user experience and ensuring that developers can effectively integrate with your API. By following the guidelines and strategies outlined in this chapter, you can create comprehensive and user-friendly documentation that contributes to the success of your API.

Chapter 10: API Versioning: Strategies and Best Practices

API versioning is an essential aspect of maintaining a robust API over time. As applications evolve, changes are inevitable—whether due to new features, bug fixes, or shifts in technology. Proper versioning allows you to make these changes without breaking existing client integrations, thus ensuring a smooth user experience and long-term stability of your API. In this chapter, we will explore the importance of API versioning, various strategies for implementing it, best practices, and real-world examples.

1. Understanding the Need for API Versioning

APIs are often consumed by multiple clients, including web applications, mobile apps, and third-party services. As these clients rely on the API for functionality, any changes that break backward compatibility can lead to significant disruptions. API versioning helps mitigate these risks by allowing developers to introduce changes in a controlled manner.

CHAPTER 10: API VERSIONING: STRATEGIES AND BEST PRACTICES

A. Key Reasons for API Versioning

1. **Backward Compatibility**: Versioning ensures that existing clients can continue to function without requiring immediate updates when changes are made to the API.
2. **Client Adaptation**: Different clients may require different features or responses. Versioning allows clients to adopt new functionality at their own pace.
3. **Controlled Change Management**: With versioning, you can manage changes more effectively, rolling out new features or deprecating old ones in a structured way.
4. **Documentation Clarity**: Each version of an API can have its own documentation, reducing confusion for developers working with different versions.

2. Strategies for API Versioning

There are several strategies for implementing API versioning, each with its pros and cons. The choice of strategy often depends on the specific requirements of your application and the preferences of your development team.

A. URI Versioning

URI versioning involves including the version number in the API endpoint's URL. This is one of the most common approaches and is straightforward to implement.

Advantages:

- Clear and explicit versioning.
- Easy to implement and understand.
- Allows for different versions to coexist.

Disadvantages:

- Can lead to URL bloat with multiple versions.
- Requires clients to update their endpoints if the version changes.

Example:

```plaintext
Copy code
GET /api/v1/users
GET /api/v2/users
```

B. Query Parameter Versioning

Another approach is to use query parameters to specify the API version. This method keeps the base URL clean and separates the versioning information from the main endpoint.

Advantages:

- Clean URL structure.
- Easy to implement without changing existing paths.

Disadvantages:

- Less explicit than URI versioning, which may confuse some developers.
- Can lead to cluttered query strings if multiple parameters are used.

Example:

```plaintext
Copy code
GET /api/users?version=1
GET /api/users?version=2
```

C. Header Versioning

With header versioning, clients specify the API version in the request headers. This method keeps URLs clean and provides flexibility for changing versions without modifying the URL structure.

Advantages:

- Clean and user-friendly URLs.
- Flexibility in managing versions without changing API paths.

Disadvantages:

- Can be less discoverable for users who are unfamiliar with the API.
- Requires clients to correctly set headers in their requests.

Example:

```http
Copy code
GET /api/users
Accept: application/vnd.yourapi.v1+json
```

D. Content Negotiation

Content negotiation allows clients to specify the version through the Accept header. This method is similar to header versioning but focuses on content types.

Advantages:

- Offers flexibility in handling different versions of the API response.
- Can support multiple formats (JSON, XML, etc.) along with versioning.

Disadvantages:

- More complex to implement and manage.
- Requires clients to understand content negotiation principles.

Example:

```http
Copy code
GET /api/users
Accept: application/json; version=1
```

E. Semantic Versioning

Semantic versioning (SemVer) involves using version numbers in a structured format (major.minor.patch). This method can be combined with any of the above strategies and provides a clear understanding of the nature of changes.

Advantages:

- Provides clear communication about the nature of changes (breaking, new features, fixes).
- Helps clients understand the impact of upgrading.

Disadvantages:

- Can be more complex to manage as versions increase.
- Requires developers to adhere to SemVer principles.

Example:

```plaintext
Copy code
GET /api/v1.0.0/users
GET /api/v2.1.0/users
```

3. Implementing API Versioning

Once you've chosen a versioning strategy, the next step is implementing it in your Flask application. This involves setting up your routes, modifying your controllers, and managing your documentation.

A. Setting Up Versioned Routes in Flask

1. **Creating Versioned Endpoints**: Use Flask's routing capabilities to define versioned endpoints. Here's how to set up versioned routes using URI versioning:

```python
Copy code
from flask import Flask, jsonify

app = Flask(__name__)

@app.route('/api/v1/users', methods=['GET'])
def get_users_v1():
    return jsonify({"users": ["Alice", "Bob"]}), 200

@app.route('/api/v2/users', methods=['GET'])
def get_users_v2():
    return jsonify({"users": [{"name": "Alice", "age": 30},
    {"name": "Bob", "age": 25}]}), 200

if __name__ == '__main__':
    app.run(debug=True)
```

1. **Routing Logic**: If you have more complex logic based on versions, consider using Flask's blueprint functionality to separate versioned routes.

```python
Copy code
from flask import Blueprint

v1 = Blueprint('v1', __name__)
v2 = Blueprint('v2', __name__)

@v1.route('/users', methods=['GET'])
def get_users_v1():
    # Implementation for version 1
    pass

@v2.route('/users', methods=['GET'])
def get_users_v2():
    # Implementation for version 2
    pass

app.register_blueprint(v1, url_prefix='/api/v1')
app.register_blueprint(v2, url_prefix='/api/v2')
```

B. Modifying Controllers for Version Handling

When implementing versioning, you may need to adjust your business logic or data models to handle changes in API responses or request formats.

1. **Conditional Logic**: In your controller functions, implement conditional logic based on the version to return the correct data format.

```python
Copy code
@app.route('/api/v2/users', methods=['GET'])
def get_users_v2():
    users = [{"name": "Alice", "age": 30}, {"name": "Bob", "age":
```

CHAPTER 10: API VERSIONING: STRATEGIES AND BEST PRACTICES

```
25}]
return jsonify(users), 200
```

1. **Data Transformation**: If you introduce new fields or change existing data structures, ensure that your controllers handle these changes appropriately.

C. Managing Deprecation

As you introduce new versions, it's important to manage the deprecation of old versions. This ensures that users are informed and can transition smoothly.

1. **Deprecation Notices**: Include deprecation notices in the API response headers or documentation.

```http
Copy code
Deprecation: version 1 will be removed on 2023-12-31
```

1. **Grace Periods**: Provide a grace period during which both the old and new versions are supported. This gives clients time to transition.
2. **Migration Guides**: Offer migration guides to help developers transition from one version to another. Include examples and explanations of what has changed.

4. Best Practices for API Versioning

Implementing API versioning effectively requires adherence to best practices that enhance usability and maintainability.

A. Consistency Across Versions

1. **Maintain Consistency**: Ensure that the behavior of endpoints remains consistent across versions. Avoid introducing breaking changes without adequate notice and a clear migration path.
2. **Document Changes**: Clearly document differences between versions, highlighting what has changed, what has been deprecated, and what new features are available.

B. Use Semantic Versioning

1. **Adopt SemVer**: Use semantic versioning to convey the significance of changes to users. For instance, increment the major version for breaking changes, the minor version for new features, and the patch version for bug fixes.
2. **Clear Versioning Scheme**: Communicate your versioning scheme clearly in your documentation to ensure users understand how to interpret version numbers.

C. Maintain Backward Compatibility

1. **Avoid Breaking Changes**: When possible, avoid breaking changes. If they are necessary, provide clear documentation and a migration path.
2. **Support Legacy Versions**: Consider maintaining legacy versions for a reasonable time, especially if clients depend on them.

D. Monitor API Usage

1. **Usage Analytics**: Implement analytics to monitor which versions of your API are in use. This information can help you make informed decisions about deprecating older versions.
2. **Feedback Loops**: Establish feedback loops with your API consumers to understand their needs and address issues with versioning.

5. Example Scenarios for API Versioning

To illustrate the concepts of API versioning, let's explore a few scenarios involving versioning decisions and their implications.

A. Scenario 1: E-Commerce API

Context: An e-commerce platform has an API that allows clients to retrieve product information, manage orders, and handle payments.

Versioning Decisions:

- **Initial Version**: The initial API version (v1) supports basic product retrieval and order management.
- **Introducing New Features**: In v2, the API introduces a new endpoint for product reviews and ratings, as well as enhanced order management features.

Implementation:

- The existing /api/v1/products endpoint continues to function without changes.
- The new /api/v2/products endpoint provides additional features while retaining backward compatibility.

Documentation:

- Document differences between versions, including the new features in v2 and how to interact with them.

B. Scenario 2: User Management API

Context: A user management API allows clients to handle user authentication and profile management.
Versioning Decisions:

- **Breaking Change**: The API decides to change the authentication mechanism from basic authentication to OAuth2 in v2.

Implementation:

- Maintain the /api/v1/login endpoint while introducing a new /api/v2/auth/login endpoint.
- Provide detailed migration documentation for clients to transition to the new authentication method.

Deprecation Notices:

- Include a deprecation notice for v1 endpoints in the responses, informing users of the upcoming removal date.

6. Conclusion

In this chapter, we explored the crucial topic of API versioning, discussing its importance in maintaining backward compatibility, managing changes, and enhancing the developer experience. We reviewed various strategies for implementing API versioning, including URI versioning, query parameter versioning, header versioning, and content negotiation.

We also covered best practices for effective versioning, such as maintaining consistency across versions, using semantic versioning, and monitoring API

CHAPTER 10: API VERSIONING: STRATEGIES AND BEST PRACTICES

usage. Through real-world examples, we illustrated the implications of versioning decisions in different scenarios.

Chapter 11: Performance Optimization for Flask APIs

Chapter 11: Performance Optimization for Flask APIs

In today's fast-paced digital landscape, performance is critical for the success of any web application, especially for APIs. Users expect quick response times, minimal latency, and reliable access to resources. As such, optimizing the performance of your Flask API is essential for providing a seamless user experience and ensuring scalability. In this chapter, we will explore various strategies and techniques for optimizing Flask API performance, including efficient database interactions, caching, asynchronous processing, and monitoring.

1. Understanding API Performance Metrics

Before diving into optimization techniques, it's important to understand the key performance metrics for APIs. By monitoring these metrics, you can identify bottlenecks and areas for improvement.

A. Key Performance Metrics

Response Time: The time it takes for the server to process a request and send a response back to the client. This is often measured in milliseconds (ms).

Throughput: The number of requests processed by the API in a given time frame (e.g., requests per second). Higher throughput indicates better performance.

Error Rate: The percentage of requests that result in errors (e.g., 4xx or 5xx HTTP status codes). A high error rate can indicate issues with the API's functionality or stability.

Latency: The time it takes for a request to travel from the client to the server and back. High latency can negatively impact user experience.

Resource Utilization: The amount of server resources (CPU, memory, disk I/O) used during API processing. Efficient resource utilization is key to scalability.

Monitoring these metrics can help you make informed decisions about optimization strategies.

  2. Optimizing Database Interactions

Database interactions are often a major source of latency in web applications. By optimizing how your Flask API interacts with the database, you can significantly improve performance.

  A. Use Connection Pooling

Connection pooling allows your application to reuse existing database connections instead of creating new ones for each request. This reduces the overhead associated with establishing new connections.

Setting Up Connection Pooling: If you're using Flask-SQLAlchemy, connection pooling is enabled by default. You can configure it using the following options:

python

Copy code

app.config['SQLALCHEMY_ENGINE_OPTIONS'] = {

'pool_size': 10,

'max_overflow': 20,

'pool_timeout': 30,

}

Benefits of Connection Pooling:

Reduces latency associated with connection establishment.

Improves throughput by reusing existing connections.

B. Optimize Queries

Inefficient queries can lead to increased response times. Here are some strategies for optimizing database queries:

Indexing: Use indexes to speed up query performance, especially on columns that are frequently used in WHERE clauses or JOIN conditions.

Example:

sql

Copy code

CREATE INDEX idx_username ON users (username);

Avoid N+1 Query Problems: Use eager loading to retrieve related data in a single query instead of issuing multiple queries.

Example:

python

Copy code

users = User.query.options(joinedload(User.profile)).all()

Use Batch Queries: Instead of making multiple individual queries, batch them together to reduce the number of round trips to the database.

Example:

python

Copy code

user_ids = [1, 2, 3]

users = User.query.filter(User.id.in_(user_ids)).all()

C. Caching Database Results

Implementing caching for frequently accessed data can greatly reduce the load on your database and improve response times.

Use Flask-Caching: Integrate Flask-Caching to cache query results.

bash

Copy code

pip install flask-caching

Example:

python

Copy code

```
from flask_caching import Cache
cache = Cache(app)
```

@cache.cached(timeout=300)

```
@app.route('/api/users')

def get_users():

users = User.query.all()

return jsonify([user.to_dict() for user in users])
```

In this example, the results of the /api/users endpoint are cached for 5 minutes.

3. Implementing Caching Strategies

Caching is one of the most effective ways to optimize API performance. By storing frequently accessed data in memory, you can reduce the number of requests to your database or external services.

A. Types of Caching

In-Memory Caching: Store data in memory for quick access. This is ideal for data that changes infrequently.

Distributed Caching: Use a distributed cache like Redis or Memcached to share cached data across multiple instances of your application.

HTTP Caching: Utilize caching mechanisms in HTTP to store responses in the client's cache, reducing the need for repeated requests.

B. Configuring Caching in Flask

Flask provides various caching libraries that can be easily integrated into your application. Here's how to set up caching using Flask-Caching with Redis:

Install Flask-Caching with Redis Support:

bash

Copy code

pip install flask-caching[redis]

Configure Flask-Caching:

python

Copy code

from flask import Flask

```
from flask_caching import Cache
```

app = Flask(__name__)

CHAPTER 11: PERFORMANCE OPTIMIZATION FOR FLASK APIS

app.config['CACHE_TYPE'] = 'RedisCache'

app.config['CACHE_REDIS_URL'] = 'redis://localhost:6379/0'

cache = Cache(app)

Cache API Responses:

python

Copy code

@cache.cached(timeout=60, query_string=True)

@app.route('/api/products')

def get_products():

products = Product.query.all()

return jsonify([product.to_dict() for product in products])

In this example, the /api/products endpoint response is cached for 60 seconds.

4. Asynchronous Processing

Asynchronous processing can improve API performance by offloading long-running tasks from the request-response cycle. By using tools like Celery, you can run tasks in the background, allowing your API to respond quickly to user requests.

A. Setting Up Celery for Asynchronous Tasks

Install Celery:

bash

Copy code

pip install celery[redis]

Basic Configuration:

python

Copy code

```
from celery import Celery
```

app = Flask(__name__)

app.config['CELERY_BROKER_URL'] = 'redis://localhost:6379/0'

```
app.config['CELERY_RESULT_BACKEND'] = 'redis://localhost:6379/0'
```

celery = Celery(app.name, broker=app.config['CELERY_BROKER_URL'])

celery.conf.update(app.config)

CHAPTER 11: PERFORMANCE OPTIMIZATION FOR FLASK APIS

Creating Background Tasks:

python

Copy code

@celery.task

def long_running_task(data):

import time

time.sleep(10) # Simulate a long-running task

```
return f"Processed {data}"
```

@app.route('/api/start-task/<data>', methods=['POST'])

def start_task(data):

task = long_running_task.apply_async(args=[data])

return jsonify({"task_id": task.id}), 202

In this example, we define a long-running task that simulates a delay and start it asynchronously.
  B. Checking Task Status

Monitor Task Progress:

python

Copy code

```
from celery.result import AsyncResult
```

@app.route('/api/task-status/<task_id>', methods=['GET'])

def task_status(task_id):

task_result = AsyncResult(task_id)

return jsonify({"task_id": task_id, "status": task_result.status}), 200

This endpoint allows clients to check the status of their background tasks.
5. Load Testing and Performance Testing

Load testing is essential for understanding how your API performs under high traffic conditions. By simulating various load scenarios, you can identify performance bottlenecks and optimize your application accordingly.

A. Tools for Load Testing

Apache JMeter: A popular open-source tool for load testing and performance measurement.

Locust: A modern, Python-based load testing tool that allows you to define user behavior in code.

Gatling: A powerful load testing framework for web applications that provides detailed metrics and reporting.

B. Conducting Load Tests

Define Test Scenarios: Identify key scenarios to test, such as user login, data retrieval, and resource-intensive operations.

Simulate Traffic: Use your chosen tool to simulate traffic patterns. For example, with Locust, you can define user behavior:

python

Copy code

```
from locust import HttpUser, task
```

class MyUser(HttpUser):

@task

def get_users(self):

self.client.get("/api/users")

Analyze Results: After running your tests, analyze the results to identify response times, error rates, and resource utilization.

6. Monitoring and Observability

Monitoring your Flask API is crucial for maintaining performance and quickly identifying issues. Implementing observability practices allows you to gain insights into your API's behavior and performance metrics.

A. Setting Up Monitoring

Use Application Performance Monitoring (APM) Tools: APM tools like New Relic, Datadog, and Sentry provide real-time monitoring of application performance and error tracking.

Integrate Logging: Use logging libraries to capture important events and errors in your application.

python

Copy code

```
import logging
logging.basicConfig(level=logging.INFO)
```

@app.route('/api/data')

def get_data():

app.logger.info("Fetching data...")

 # Fetch data logic

return jsonify(data)

Monitor Key Metrics: Track key performance metrics such as response times, throughput, and error rates using monitoring tools or custom dashboards.

B. Alerting and Notifications

Set Up Alerts: Configure alerts for critical metrics (e.g., high error rates or slow response times) to ensure timely intervention when issues arise.

Use Logging as a Service: Consider using services like Loggly or Splunk to aggregate and analyze logs from your application.

7. Conclusion

In this chapter, we explored various strategies for optimizing the performance of your Flask API. We began by discussing the key performance metrics that are critical for assessing API performance and identified ways to optimize database interactions through connection pooling, query optimization, and caching.

We also covered the importance of asynchronous processing for handling long-running tasks and how to set up Celery for background task management. Load testing was emphasized as a vital component for understanding how your API performs under stress, and we discussed tools and methodologies for conducting effective load tests.

Finally, we highlighted the significance of monitoring and observability in maintaining the health of your API, ensuring that you can identify and address performance issues proactively.

By implementing these optimization techniques, you can enhance the performance, scalability, and reliability of your Flask API, ultimately delivering a better experience for your users. In the next chapter, we will delve into strategies for improving API security, exploring common vulnerabilities, authentication mechanisms, and best practices for securing your API endpoints. This knowledge will be critical for protecting your application and user data in an increasingly interconnected world.

In today's fast-paced digital landscape, performance is critical for the success of any web application, especially for APIs. Users expect quick response times, minimal latency, and reliable access to resources. As such, optimizing the performance of your Flask API is essential for providing a seamless user experience and ensuring scalability. In this chapter, we will explore various strategies and techniques for optimizing Flask API performance, including efficient database interactions, caching, asynchronous processing, and monitoring.

1. Understanding API Performance Metrics

Before diving into optimization techniques, it's important to understand the key performance metrics for APIs. By monitoring these metrics, you can identify bottlenecks and areas for improvement.

A. Key Performance Metrics

1. **Response Time**: The time it takes for the server to process a request and send a response back to the client. This is often measured in milliseconds (ms).
2. **Throughput**: The number of requests processed by the API in a given time frame (e.g., requests per second). Higher throughput indicates better performance.
3. **Error Rate**: The percentage of requests that result in errors (e.g., 4xx or 5xx HTTP status codes). A high error rate can indicate issues with the API's functionality or stability.

4. **Latency**: The time it takes for a request to travel from the client to the server and back. High latency can negatively impact user experience.
5. **Resource Utilization**: The amount of server resources (CPU, memory, disk I/O) used during API processing. Efficient resource utilization is key to scalability.

Monitoring these metrics can help you make informed decisions about optimization strategies.

2. Optimizing Database Interactions

Database interactions are often a major source of latency in web applications. By optimizing how your Flask API interacts with the database, you can significantly improve performance.

A. Use Connection Pooling

Connection pooling allows your application to reuse existing database connections instead of creating new ones for each request. This reduces the overhead associated with establishing new connections.

1. **Setting Up Connection Pooling**: If you're using Flask-SQLAlchemy, connection pooling is enabled by default. You can configure it using the following options:

```python
Copy code
app.config['SQLALCHEMY_ENGINE_OPTIONS'] = {
    'pool_size': 10,
    'max_overflow': 20,
    'pool_timeout': 30,
}
```

1. **Benefits of Connection Pooling**:

- Reduces latency associated with connection establishment.

- Improves throughput by reusing existing connections.

B. Optimize Queries

Inefficient queries can lead to increased response times. Here are some strategies for optimizing database queries:

1. **Indexing**: Use indexes to speed up query performance, especially on columns that are frequently used in WHERE clauses or JOIN conditions.
2. **Example**:

```sql
Copy code
CREATE INDEX idx_username ON users (username);
```

1. **Avoid N+1 Query Problems**: Use eager loading to retrieve related data in a single query instead of issuing multiple queries.
2. **Example**:

```python
Copy code
users = User.query.options(joinedload(User.profile)).all()
```

1. **Use Batch Queries**: Instead of making multiple individual queries, batch them together to reduce the number of round trips to the database.
2. **Example**:

```python
Copy code
user_ids = [1, 2, 3]
users = User.query.filter(User.id.in_(user_ids)).all()
```

C. Caching Database Results

Implementing caching for frequently accessed data can greatly reduce the load on your database and improve response times.

1. **Use Flask-Caching**: Integrate Flask-Caching to cache query results.

```bash
Copy code
pip install flask-caching
```

Example:

```python
Copy code
from flask_caching import Cache

cache = Cache(app)

@cache.cached(timeout=300)
@app.route('/api/users')
def get_users():
    users = User.query.all()
    return jsonify([user.to_dict() for user in users])
```

In this example, the results of the /api/users endpoint are cached for 5 minutes.

3. Implementing Caching Strategies

Caching is one of the most effective ways to optimize API performance. By storing frequently accessed data in memory, you can reduce the number of requests to your database or external services.

A. Types of Caching

1. **In-Memory Caching**: Store data in memory for quick access. This is ideal for data that changes infrequently.
2. **Distributed Caching**: Use a distributed cache like Redis or Memcached to share cached data across multiple instances of your application.
3. **HTTP Caching**: Utilize caching mechanisms in HTTP to store responses in the client's cache, reducing the need for repeated requests.

B. Configuring Caching in Flask

Flask provides various caching libraries that can be easily integrated into your application. Here's how to set up caching using Flask-Caching with Redis:

1. **Install Flask-Caching with Redis Support**:

```bash
Copy code
pip install flask-caching[redis]
```

1. **Configure Flask-Caching**:

```python
Copy code
from flask import Flask
from flask_caching import Cache

app = Flask(__name__)
```

CHAPTER 11: PERFORMANCE OPTIMIZATION FOR FLASK APIS

```
app.config['CACHE_TYPE'] = 'RedisCache'
app.config['CACHE_REDIS_URL'] = 'redis://localhost:6379/0'
cache = Cache(app)
```

1. **Cache API Responses**:

```python
Copy code
@cache.cached(timeout=60, query_string=True)
@app.route('/api/products')
def get_products():
    products = Product.query.all()
    return jsonify([product.to_dict() for product in products])
```

In this example, the /api/products endpoint response is cached for 60 seconds.

4. Asynchronous Processing

Asynchronous processing can improve API performance by offloading long-running tasks from the request-response cycle. By using tools like Celery, you can run tasks in the background, allowing your API to respond quickly to user requests.

A. Setting Up Celery for Asynchronous Tasks

1. **Install Celery**:

```bash
Copy code
pip install celery[redis]
```

1. **Basic Configuration**:

```python
Copy code
from celery import Celery

app = Flask(__name__)
app.config['CELERY_BROKER_URL'] = 'redis://localhost:6379/0'
app.config['CELERY_RESULT_BACKEND'] = 'redis://localhost:6379/0'

celery = Celery(app.name, broker=app.config['CELERY_BROKER_URL'])
celery.conf.update(app.config)
```

1. **Creating Background Tasks**:

```python
Copy code
@celery.task
def long_running_task(data):
    import time
    time.sleep(10)  # Simulate a long-running task
    return f"Processed {data}"

@app.route('/api/start-task/<data>', methods=['POST'])
def start_task(data):
    task = long_running_task.apply_async(args=[data])
    return jsonify({"task_id": task.id}), 202
```

In this example, we define a long-running task that simulates a delay and start it asynchronously.

B. Checking Task Status

1. **Monitor Task Progress**:

CHAPTER 11: PERFORMANCE OPTIMIZATION FOR FLASK APIS

```python
Copy code
from celery.result import AsyncResult

@app.route('/api/task-status/<task_id>', methods=['GET'])
def task_status(task_id):
    task_result = AsyncResult(task_id)
    return jsonify({"task_id": task_id, "status":
    task_result.status}), 200
```

This endpoint allows clients to check the status of their background tasks.

5. Load Testing and Performance Testing

Load testing is essential for understanding how your API performs under high traffic conditions. By simulating various load scenarios, you can identify performance bottlenecks and optimize your application accordingly.

A. Tools for Load Testing

1. **Apache JMeter**: A popular open-source tool for load testing and performance measurement.
2. **Locust**: A modern, Python-based load testing tool that allows you to define user behavior in code.
3. **Gatling**: A powerful load testing framework for web applications that provides detailed metrics and reporting.

B. Conducting Load Tests

1. **Define Test Scenarios**: Identify key scenarios to test, such as user login, data retrieval, and resource-intensive operations.
2. **Simulate Traffic**: Use your chosen tool to simulate traffic patterns. For example, with Locust, you can define user behavior:

```python
Copy code
from locust import HttpUser, task

class MyUser(HttpUser):
    @task
    def get_users(self):
        self.client.get("/api/users")
```

1. **Analyze Results**: After running your tests, analyze the results to identify response times, error rates, and resource utilization.

6. Monitoring and Observability

Monitoring your Flask API is crucial for maintaining performance and quickly identifying issues. Implementing observability practices allows you to gain insights into your API's behavior and performance metrics.

A. Setting Up Monitoring

1. **Use Application Performance Monitoring (APM) Tools**: APM tools like New Relic, Datadog, and Sentry provide real-time monitoring of application performance and error tracking.
2. **Integrate Logging**: Use logging libraries to capture important events and errors in your application.

```python
Copy code
import logging

logging.basicConfig(level=logging.INFO)

@app.route('/api/data')
def get_data():
    app.logger.info("Fetching data...")
```

CHAPTER 11: PERFORMANCE OPTIMIZATION FOR FLASK APIS

```
# Fetch data logic
return jsonify(data)
```

1. **Monitor Key Metrics**: Track key performance metrics such as response times, throughput, and error rates using monitoring tools or custom dashboards.

B. Alerting and Notifications

1. **Set Up Alerts**: Configure alerts for critical metrics (e.g., high error rates or slow response times) to ensure timely intervention when issues arise.
2. **Use Logging as a Service**: Consider using services like Loggly or Splunk to aggregate and analyze logs from your application.

7. Conclusion

In this chapter, we explored various strategies for optimizing the performance of your Flask API. We began by discussing the key performance metrics that are critical for assessing API performance and identified ways to optimize database interactions through connection pooling, query optimization, and caching.

We also covered the importance of asynchronous processing for handling long-running tasks and how to set up Celery for background task management. Load testing was emphasized as a vital component for understanding how your API performs under stress, and we discussed tools and methodologies for conducting effective load tests.

Finally, we highlighted the significance of monitoring and observability in maintaining the health of your API, ensuring that you can identify and address performance issues proactively.

By implementing these optimization techniques, you can enhance the performance, scalability, and reliability of your Flask API, ultimately delivering a better experience for your users. In the next chapter, we will delve into strategies for improving API security, exploring common vulnerabilities, authentication mechanisms, and best practices for securing your API endpoints. This knowledge will be critical for protecting your application and user data in an increasingly interconnected world.

Chapter 12: Securing Your Flask API: Best Practices and Strategies

Chapter 12: Securing Your Flask API: Best Practices and Strategies

In an era where data breaches and cyberattacks are increasingly common, securing your API is paramount. A well-secured API not only protects sensitive data but also builds trust with users and partners. This chapter will delve into the various strategies and best practices for securing your Flask API, including authentication methods, authorization mechanisms, data validation, protection against common vulnerabilities, and monitoring and logging for security purposes.

1. Understanding API Security

API security encompasses a wide range of practices aimed at protecting the integrity, confidentiality, and availability of your API. APIs can be exposed to various threats, including unauthorized access, data manipulation, and denial-of-service attacks. Understanding these threats is the first step toward implementing effective security measures.

A. Common Threats to APIs

Unauthorized Access: Attackers attempting to access restricted resources or data without proper credentials can lead to data breaches.

Data Manipulation: Malicious users may try to manipulate data transmitted to or from the API, affecting application functionality and integrity.

Injection Attacks: Techniques like SQL injection, where malicious code is injected into a request, can compromise the security of your database.

Cross-Site Scripting (XSS): Attackers may attempt to inject malicious scripts into responses sent by your API, leading to unauthorized actions on behalf of users.

Denial-of-Service (DoS) Attacks: Flooding your API with excessive requests can lead to service downtime, affecting availability.

2. Authentication and Authorization

Authentication and authorization are fundamental components of API security. They ensure that only legitimate users have access to your API and its resources.

A. Authentication Methods

API Keys: A simple form of authentication where clients include a unique API key in their requests. While easy to implement, API keys can be less secure as they can be easily shared or leaked.

CHAPTER 12: SECURING YOUR FLASK API: BEST PRACTICES AND...

Example:

python

Copy code

```
from flask import request, jsonify
```

@app.route('/api/resource', methods=['GET'])

def get_resource():

api_key = request.headers.get('Authorization')

if api_key != 'your_api_key':

return jsonify({"message": "Unauthorized"}), 401

Process request

Bearer Tokens: A more secure method where clients authenticate using a token, typically obtained through an initial login process. Bearer tokens are commonly used with OAuth2.

Example:

python

Copy code

from flask import request, jsonify

```
from flask_jwt_extended import JWTManager, jwt_required
jwt = JWTManager(app)
```

@app.route('/api/protected', methods=['GET'])

@jwt_required()

def protected():

return jsonify({"message": "You have access to this resource!"}), 200

OAuth2: An industry-standard protocol for authorization that allows third-party applications to obtain limited access to user accounts. OAuth2 involves the use of access tokens and refresh tokens.

Example:

python

Copy code

@app.route('/api/oauth', methods=['POST'])

```python
def oauth_login():
    # Validate user credentials and generate tokens
    return jsonify({"access_token": "your_access_token"}), 200
```

B. Authorization Mechanisms

Authorization ensures that authenticated users have the appropriate permissions to access specific resources.

Role-Based Access Control (RBAC): Users are assigned roles, and permissions are granted based on those roles. This method simplifies management by grouping permissions.

Example:

python

Copy code

```python
@app.route('/api/admin', methods=['GET'])
@jwt_required()
def admin_resource():
    current_user = get_jwt_identity()
    if not user_has_role(current_user, 'admin'):
```

return jsonify({"message": "Forbidden"}), 403

return jsonify({"message": "Welcome to the admin area!"}), 200

Attribute-Based Access Control (ABAC): Authorization is based on user attributes and environmental conditions. This method offers more granular control compared to RBAC.

Example:

python

Copy code

def can_access_resource(user, resource):

Custom logic to determine access based on user attributes

return user.role == 'admin' or user.department == resource.department

3. Data Validation and Sanitization
   Data validation and sanitization are critical for preventing attacks such as SQL injection and XSS.
   A. Input Validation

Use Schema Validation: Validate incoming data against predefined schemas to ensure that the data conforms to expected formats.

Example with Marshmallow:

python

Copy code

```
from marshmallow import Schema, fields, ValidationError
```

class UserSchema(Schema):

username = fields.Str(required=True)

```
password = fields.Str(required=True)
```

@app.route('/api/users', methods=['POST'])

def create_user():

try:

user_schema = UserSchema()

user_data = user_schema.load(request.json)

Process user creation

except ValidationError as err:

return jsonify(err.messages), 400

Whitelist Valid Values: When expecting specific values, use whitelisting to ensure only valid data is accepted.

Example:

python

Copy code

valid_roles = ['admin', 'user', 'guest']

if data['role'] not in valid_roles:

return jsonify({"message": "Invalid role"}), 400

B. Output Sanitization

Sanitize Output: Clean any data sent to clients to prevent XSS attacks.

Example with Bleach:

python

Copy code

```
from bleach import clean
```

@app.route('/api/comments', methods=['POST'])

```python
def add_comment():

    comment = request.json.get('comment')

    sanitized_comment = clean(comment)

    # Save sanitized comment
```

4. Protection Against Common Vulnerabilities

APIs are often vulnerable to various attacks. Here are some strategies for mitigating common vulnerabilities.

  A. Cross-Site Scripting (XSS)

Content Security Policy (CSP): Implement CSP headers to control which resources can be loaded by the client. This helps prevent the execution of malicious scripts.

Example:

python

Copy code

```python
@app.after_request

def apply_csp(response):

    response.headers['Content-Security-Policy'] = "default-src 'self'"

    return response
```

Output Encoding: Ensure that all output is encoded properly to prevent XSS.

B. SQL Injection

Use ORM: Use an Object-Relational Mapping (ORM) library like SQLAlchemy to handle database interactions. ORMs automatically escape inputs, reducing the risk of SQL injection.

Example:

python

Copy code

user = User.query.filter_by(username=username).first() # Safe from injection

Parameterized Queries: If you must use raw SQL queries, ensure that they are parameterized.

Example:

python

Copy code

cursor.execute("SELECT * FROM users WHERE username = %s", (username,))

C. Cross-Site Request Forgery (CSRF)

CSRF Protection: Use CSRF tokens to protect against CSRF attacks. Flask-WTF provides built-in CSRF protection.

Example:

python

Copy code

```
from flask_wtf.csrf import CSRFProtect
```

csrf = CSRFProtect(app)

Check Referer Header: Optionally, validate the Referer header to ensure that requests originate from allowed domains.

5. Monitoring and Logging for Security
   Implementing monitoring and logging practices is crucial for detecting and responding to security incidents.
   A. Set Up Logging

Use a Structured Logging Framework: Utilize a structured logging framework to capture security-relevant events. Python's built-in logging module can be configured for this purpose.

Example:

python

Copy code

```
import logging
logging.basicConfig(level=logging.INFO)
```

@app.route('/api/login', methods=['POST'])

def login():

username = request.json.get('username')

Log login attempts

app.logger.info(f"Login attempt by user: {username}")

Log Sensitive Actions: Log significant actions, such as failed login attempts or data changes, but ensure that sensitive information is not logged.

B. Implement Intrusion Detection

Monitor for Anomalous Behavior: Set up alerts for unusual activities, such as multiple failed login attempts or unexpected API usage patterns.

Use Security Information and Event Management (SIEM) Tools: Consider integrating with SIEM tools to aggregate logs and analyze them for potential security threats.

6. Secure API Deployment

Once your Flask API is built and secured, consider the following practices for secure deployment:

A. Use HTTPS

Encrypt Data in Transit: Use HTTPS to encrypt all data transmitted between clients and your API. This protects against man-in-the-middle attacks.

Obtain SSL Certificates: Use trusted Certificate Authorities (CAs) to obtain SSL certificates for your domain.

B. Rate Limiting

Limit API Requests: Implement rate limiting to prevent abuse of your API, which can help mitigate denial-of-service attacks.

Example with Flask-Limiter:

bash

Copy code

pip install flask-limiter

python

Copy code

```
from flask_limiter import Limiter
limiter = Limiter(app, key_func=get_remote_address)
```

@limiter.limit("5 per minute")

@app.route('/api/resource')

def resource():

return jsonify({"message": "This is a rate-limited resource."})

C. Secure Configuration

Environment Variables: Store sensitive configuration values (e.g., API keys, database passwords) in environment variables rather than hardcoding them in your application.

Configuration Management Tools: Use configuration management tools like Ansible, Chef, or Puppet to manage server configurations securely.

7. Best Practices for Securing Your Flask API

To enhance the security of your Flask API, consider implementing the following best practices:

Follow the Principle of Least Privilege: Grant only the permissions necessary for users and systems to perform their tasks.

Regularly Update Dependencies: Keep your Flask application and its dependencies updated to protect against known vulnerabilities.

Conduct Security Audits: Regularly perform security audits and penetration testing to identify vulnerabilities and assess your API's security posture.

Educate Your Team: Provide training for your development and operations teams on secure coding practices and API security principles.

Implement API Gateway: Consider using an API gateway that provides built-in security features, such as rate limiting, authentication, and logging.

8. Conclusion

In this chapter, we explored the critical aspects of securing your Flask API. We began by discussing the importance of API security and common threats that APIs face. We covered various authentication and authorization methods, including API keys, bearer tokens, and OAuth2, as well as best practices for data validation and sanitization.

We also addressed protection against common vulnerabilities such as XSS, SQL injection, and CSRF, emphasizing the importance of monitoring and logging for security purposes. Finally, we discussed secure deployment practices, including the use of HTTPS, rate limiting, and secure configuration management.

By implementing these strategies and best practices, you can significantly enhance the security of your Flask API, protect sensitive data, and foster trust with your users. In the next chapter, we will explore the topic of API documentation in greater detail, focusing on best practices for creating comprehensive and user-friendly documentation that enables developers to effectively utilize your API. This knowledge will be essential for ensuring that your API is accessible and easy to understand for its users.

Chapter 13: Effective API Documentation: Best Practices and Tools

API documentation is critical for the success of any API. It serves as the primary resource for developers who wish to understand and integrate with your API, detailing everything from authentication methods to endpoint descriptions and usage examples. Well-crafted documentation not only enhances user experience but also minimizes support requests and drives adoption. In this chapter, we will explore the best practices for creating effective API documentation, the tools available to assist in this process, and provide a structured approach to organizing your documentation for clarity and accessibility.

1. The Importance of API Documentation

API documentation is often the first interaction developers have with your API. It can significantly influence their decision to use your API over others. Clear, concise, and comprehensive documentation can lead to higher adoption rates, reduced friction in integration, and improved developer satisfaction.

A. Benefits of Well-Written API Documentation

1. **Ease of Integration**: Clear documentation helps developers quickly understand how to integrate with your API, reducing the time to market for their applications.
2. **Reduced Support Burden**: Good documentation can answer common questions and issues, leading to fewer support requests and allowing your team to focus on higher-value tasks.
3. **Improved Developer Experience**: Developers are more likely to have a positive experience when they can easily find the information they need, which can lead to increased loyalty to your API.
4. **Facilitates Collaboration**: Comprehensive documentation fosters better collaboration among teams by providing a common understanding of how the API works.
5. **Documentation for Maintenance**: As APIs evolve, maintaining clear documentation helps ensure that changes are communicated effectively, preventing disruptions to existing clients.

2. Principles of Effective API Documentation

Creating effective API documentation requires adherence to several key principles that ensure clarity, usability, and accessibility.

A. Clarity and Simplicity

1. **Use Clear Language**: Avoid technical jargon and write in simple, straightforward language. The goal is to communicate effectively with developers of varying experience levels.
2. **Be Consistent**: Use consistent terminology and formatting throughout your documentation. This consistency helps reduce confusion and improves comprehension.
3. **Logical Structure**: Organize your documentation logically, grouping related information together. Use headings and subheadings to guide

readers through the material.

B. Comprehensive Coverage

1. **Endpoint Descriptions**: Provide detailed descriptions of each API endpoint, including the method (GET, POST, etc.), URL, parameters, request body, and expected responses.
2. **Authentication Methods**: Clearly explain how to authenticate with the API, detailing required tokens, API keys, or OAuth flows.
3. **Error Handling**: Document possible error responses, including status codes, error messages, and suggested resolutions.

C. Visual Aids

1. **Code Samples**: Include code snippets to demonstrate how to use the API effectively. Provide examples in multiple programming languages when possible.
2. **Diagrams and Flowcharts**: Use visual aids to clarify complex processes, such as authentication flows or data interactions.
3. **Interactive Documentation**: Utilize tools that allow users to interact with the API directly from the documentation, enabling them to test endpoints without leaving the page.

3. Tools for API Documentation

Several tools can help streamline the process of creating, managing, and publishing API documentation. Below are some popular options:

A. Swagger/OpenAPI

Overview: Swagger is a framework for API documentation that utilizes the OpenAPI Specification (OAS) to describe RESTful APIs. It provides an interactive interface for developers to explore APIs.

Key Features:

- Generate interactive API documentation that developers can use to test endpoints.
- Support for various programming languages and frameworks.
- Ability to define request/response formats, authentication methods, and error codes.

Example Setup: To use Swagger with a Flask application, you can utilize the flasgger extension:

1. **Installation**:

```bash
Copy code
pip install flasgger
```

1. **Basic Configuration**:

```python
Copy code
from flask import Flask
from flasgger import Swagger

app = Flask(__name__)
swagger = Swagger(app)

@app.route('/api/users', methods=['GET'])
def get_users():
    """
    Retrieve a list of users.
    ---
```

```
      responses:
        200:
          description: A list of users
          schema:
            type: array
            items:
              type: object
              properties:
                id:
                  type: integer
                  example: 1
                username:
                  type: string
                  example: testuser
    """
    users = [{"id": 1, "username": "testuser"}]
    return jsonify(users), 200
```

B. Postman

Overview: Postman is a versatile tool for API development that includes functionality for documenting APIs. It allows you to create collections of requests and provides an interface for testing and sharing APIs.

Key Features:

- Create documentation directly from Postman collections.
- Share collections and documentation with team members or the public.
- Generate code snippets for different programming languages.

Example Setup:

1. Create a collection of requests in Postman.
2. Use the documentation feature to add descriptions, examples, and notes for each request.
3. Publish the documentation for easy access.

C. Read the Docs

Overview: Read the Docs is a platform that hosts documentation for open-source projects. It supports Markdown and reStructuredText formats, making it easy to write and publish documentation.

Key Features:

- Automatic builds of documentation from your repository.
- Versioning support to maintain documentation for different API versions.
- Search functionality for easy navigation.

Example Setup:

1. Write your documentation in Markdown or reStructuredText format.
2. Configure Read the Docs to build your documentation from your version control system (e.g., GitHub).
3. Publish and share the documentation with users.

4. Structuring Your API Documentation

A well-structured API documentation is crucial for usability. Below is a recommended structure for organizing your documentation:

A. Overview

- **Introduction**: Provide a brief overview of your API, its purpose, and the problems it solves.
- **Getting Started**: Include instructions for obtaining access to the API (e.g., signing up for an API key) and an overview of the authentication process.

B. Authentication

- **Authentication Methods**: Detail the authentication methods supported by your API (e.g., API keys, OAuth2).
- **Example Authentication Flow**: Provide examples of how to authenticate and include sample requests.

C. API Endpoints

- **Endpoint Structure**: For each endpoint, include the following sections:
- **Endpoint URL**: The URL for the endpoint.
- **HTTP Method**: The HTTP method used (GET, POST, etc.).
- **Parameters**: Describe any query parameters or path parameters required for the request.
- **Request Body**: Provide details on the request body, including required and optional fields.
- **Response Format**: Document the expected response format, including success and error responses.
- **Examples**: Include code snippets demonstrating how to interact with the endpoint.

D. Error Handling

- **Error Codes**: List all possible error codes and their meanings.
- **Error Responses**: Provide examples of error responses, including sample messages.

E. Rate Limiting and Quotas

- **Usage Limits**: Explain any rate limits or quotas imposed on the API and how users can monitor their usage.
- **Handling Rate Limit Errors**: Provide guidance on how to handle rate limit errors when they occur.

F. Additional Resources

- **SDKs and Libraries**: If available, provide links to SDKs or libraries that simplify integration with your API.
- **Support and Contact Information**: Include information on how users can reach out for support or report issues.

5. Writing API Documentation

Writing effective API documentation involves clarity, conciseness, and thoroughness. Here are some tips for writing high-quality documentation:

A. Use Simple Language

1. **Avoid Jargon**: Use language that is easily understandable by developers of varying expertise levels. Avoid technical jargon unless necessary, and define any specialized terms.
2. **Be Direct**: Use a straightforward writing style that conveys information clearly. Avoid unnecessary fluff or overly complex sentences.

B. Provide Clear Examples

1. **Code Samples**: Include code samples that demonstrate how to use the API effectively. Use a variety of programming languages to cater to a broader audience.
2. **Request/Response Examples**: Provide examples of actual requests and responses for each endpoint, including both successful and error scenarios.

C. Keep Documentation Up to Date

1. **Version Control**: Maintain documentation versions to reflect changes in the API. Ensure that users can access the documentation for the specific version of the API they are using.
2. **Regular Reviews**: Schedule regular reviews of your documentation to ensure it remains accurate and up to date. Encourage team members to report discrepancies or suggest improvements.

6. Example of Comprehensive API Documentation

To illustrate the principles discussed, here is a structured example of API documentation for a fictional user management API:

User Management API Documentation

Overview

The User Management API provides endpoints for managing user accounts, including registration, authentication, and profile management.

Getting Started

To use the User Management API, sign up for an API key at [yourwebsite.com/signup]. Once you have your API key, include it in the Authorization header for all requests.

Authentication

The User Management API uses API key-based authentication. Include your API key in the header of each request.
    Example:

```
http
Copy code
Authorization: Bearer your_api_key_here
```

API Endpoints

1. User Registration

- **Endpoint URL**: /api/users/register
- **HTTP Method**: POST
- **Request Body**:
  - username (string, required): The username for the new user.
  - password (string, required): The password for the new user.

Example Request:

```json
Copy code
{
  "username": "newuser",
  "password": "password123"
}
```

Response:

- **201 Created**: User registered successfully.
- **409 Conflict**: Username already exists.

Example Response:

```json
Copy code
```

```
{
  "message": "User registered successfully."
}
```

2. User Authentication

- **Endpoint URL**: /api/users/login
- **HTTP Method**: POST
- **Request Body**:
- username (string, required): The username of the user.
- password (string, required): The password of the user.

Example Request:

```json
Copy code
{
  "username": "newuser",
  "password": "password123"
}
```

Response:

- **200 OK**: Authentication successful, returns a JWT token.
- **401 Unauthorized**: Invalid credentials.

Example Response:

```json
Copy code
{
  "token": "your_jwt_token_here"
}
```

Error Handling

Status CodeDescription
400
Bad Request: Invalid input data
401
Unauthorized: Invalid credentials
409
Conflict: Resource already exists
500
Internal Server Error: Unexpected error

Rate Limiting

The User Management API enforces rate limiting to prevent abuse. Users are limited to 100 requests per hour. Exceeding this limit will result in a 429 Too Many Requests response.

Example Error Response:

```json
Copy code
{
   "error": "Too Many Requests",
   "message": "You have exceeded the rate limit."
}
```

Additional Resources

- SDK for Python
- SDK for JavaScript

Support

For support, please contact our support team at support@yourwebsite.com or visit our support page.

7. Tools and Technologies for API Documentation

There are several tools and technologies that can assist you in creating effective API documentation. Below are some popular options and their key features:

A. Swagger/OpenAPI

- **Interactive Documentation**: Automatically generate interactive documentation that allows developers to test API endpoints.
- **API Specification**: Use the OpenAPI Specification to define your API's endpoints, request/response formats, and authentication methods.

B. Postman

- **API Testing and Documentation**: Create collections of requests and use them to generate documentation.
- **Code Generation**: Postman can generate code snippets in various programming languages for easy integration.

C. Read the Docs

- **Host Documentation**: Read the Docs hosts documentation for open-source projects and can automatically build it from your repository.
- **Version Control**: Supports versioning, allowing you to maintain documentation for different API versions.

D. Markdown and Static Site Generators

- **Markdown**: Write documentation in Markdown format for simplicity and ease of use.
- **Static Site Generators**: Use tools like Jekyll or Hugo to generate static documentation sites from Markdown files.

8. Conclusion

In this chapter, we explored the critical aspects of API documentation, emphasizing the importance of clarity, comprehensiveness, and usability. We discussed various tools available for creating and managing documentation, including Swagger, Postman, and Read the Docs, and provided a structured approach for organizing your documentation effectively.

We also highlighted best practices for writing high-quality documentation, including using simple language, providing clear examples, and keeping documentation up to date.

By investing time and effort into creating excellent API documentation, you can enhance the developer experience, drive adoption, and ultimately contribute to the success of your API. In the next chapter, we will explore strategies for handling API deprecation and sunset policies, ensuring that your users have a smooth transition when changes occur in your API offerings. This knowledge will be essential for maintaining a positive relationship with your API consumers while evolving your services.

Chapter 14: Managing API Deprecation and Sunset Policies

As APIs evolve, there will inevitably be changes that require the deprecation of older versions or endpoints. Deprecation refers to the process of marking an API endpoint as obsolete, typically in preparation for its eventual removal. Effectively managing API deprecation and implementing a sunset policy is crucial for maintaining trust with your users, ensuring a smooth transition to newer versions, and minimizing disruptions. In this chapter, we will explore the strategies for managing API deprecation, best practices for communicating changes to users, and effective sunset policies to phase out deprecated APIs gracefully.

1. Understanding API Deprecation

API deprecation is a common part of the API lifecycle, allowing developers to introduce improvements and new features without breaking existing integrations. However, how you manage deprecation can significantly impact your users and the overall success of your API.

A. Reasons for API Deprecation

1. **Improvements in Functionality**: As the technology landscape evolves, APIs may need to change to incorporate better practices, enhanced functionality, or improved performance.
2. **Security Enhancements**: Older APIs may have security vulnerabilities that require deprecation in favor of more secure alternatives.
3. **Obsolescence**: Certain features or endpoints may become outdated due to changing business requirements or technology advancements.
4. **User Feedback**: Developers may find that certain API features are rarely used or cause confusion, prompting a review and potential deprecation.

B. Consequences of Poor Deprecation Management

1. **User Frustration**: If users are not adequately informed about deprecated features, they may encounter unexpected errors or disruptions in their applications.
2. **Increased Support Burden**: Poor communication regarding deprecation can lead to a spike in support requests, as users struggle to adapt to the changes.
3. **Loss of Trust**: Users may lose trust in your API if they feel that changes are made arbitrarily without consideration for their needs.

2. Strategies for Managing API Deprecation

Implementing a structured approach to API deprecation is essential for minimizing disruptions and ensuring a smooth transition for users. Here are some key strategies for effectively managing API deprecation.

CHAPTER 14: MANAGING API DEPRECATION AND SUNSET POLICIES

A. *Clear Versioning and Change Management*

1. **Semantic Versioning**: Adopt semantic versioning to communicate the nature of changes clearly. For instance, increment the major version number for breaking changes, the minor version for new features, and the patch version for bug fixes.
2. **Versioning Strategy**: Clearly define your versioning strategy, including how you will communicate changes, deprecations, and sunset policies. Document this strategy in your API documentation.

B. *Deprecation Notices*

1. **Communicate Changes**: Notify users well in advance of any deprecation plans. Use multiple channels to communicate this information, such as email newsletters, blog posts, and documentation updates.
2. **Include Deprecation Warnings**: Include deprecation warnings in API responses for deprecated endpoints, informing users that they should migrate to a newer version.

Example:

```
json
Copy code
{
  "error": "Deprecated",
  "message": "This endpoint will be removed on 2023-12-31. Please migrate to /api/v2/users."
}
```

C. Grace Period

1. **Provide a Transition Period**: Offer a grace period during which both the old and new versions of the API are supported. This allows users time to transition without service interruption.
2. **Monitor Usage**: Track the usage of deprecated endpoints during the grace period. This information can help you understand how many users are affected and tailor your communication accordingly.

D. Migration Guides

1. **Provide Comprehensive Migration Guides**: Create detailed migration guides that outline the differences between the deprecated and new versions. Include examples, code snippets, and common pitfalls to avoid.
2. **Highlight Benefits**: Clearly communicate the benefits of the new version or endpoint to encourage users to make the transition.

3. Best Practices for Communicating Deprecation

Effective communication is key to ensuring a smooth transition during the deprecation process. Here are best practices for communicating changes to your users.

A. Multi-Channel Communication

1. **Email Notifications**: Send direct email notifications to registered users about upcoming deprecations and changes to the API.
2. **Developer Portals**: Update your developer portal or website with announcements regarding deprecation and migration information.
3. **Social Media**: Use social media platforms to inform users about changes and direct them to relevant resources.

CHAPTER 14: MANAGING API DEPRECATION AND SUNSET POLICIES

B. Documentation Updates

1. **Versioned Documentation**: Maintain separate documentation for each version of your API, clearly indicating deprecated features and their replacements.
2. **Deprecation Section**: Create a dedicated section in your documentation to detail all deprecated endpoints, including timelines for removal and migration paths.

C. User Feedback Loop

1. **Encourage Feedback**: Provide users with a way to submit feedback on the deprecation process and any challenges they encounter during migration.
2. **Engage with the Community**: Participate in community forums and support channels to address concerns and assist users in adapting to changes.

4. Implementing Sunset Policies

Sunset policies define the process for phasing out deprecated APIs or endpoints. A well-defined sunset policy ensures that users have a clear understanding of when deprecated features will be removed and what steps they need to take.

A. Defining Sunset Timelines

1. **Establish Clear Timelines**: Set clear timelines for the deprecation process, including when deprecation notices will be sent, the length of the grace period, and the final removal date.
2. **Communicate Timelines**: Ensure that timelines are communicated effectively across all channels and that users are reminded as key dates approach.

B. Phased Approach to Removal

1. **Gradual Phase-Out**: Consider a phased approach to removing deprecated features, where you first disable non-critical functionality before removing core features.
2. **Monitor Impact**: During the phased removal process, monitor the impact on users and address any concerns promptly.

C. Continuous Improvement

1. **Review Feedback**: After implementing sunset policies, review user feedback and assess the effectiveness of your communication and support strategies.
2. **Adjust Policies as Needed**: Based on feedback and lessons learned, be prepared to adjust your deprecation and sunset policies for future changes.

5. Real-World Examples of API Deprecation Management

To illustrate effective deprecation management, let's examine real-world examples of how companies have successfully navigated the deprecation process.

A. Example 1: Twitter API Deprecation

Context: Twitter has undergone several API version changes over the years, deprecating older versions of its API while introducing new features and improvements.
Strategies Used:

- **Clear Communication**: Twitter communicated changes through its developer blog, email notifications, and status updates.
- **Migration Guides**: Comprehensive migration guides were provided to

help developers transition to new endpoints.
- **Grace Periods**: Twitter offered a grace period during which both old and new API versions were available.

B. Example 2: Facebook Graph API

Context: Facebook regularly updates its Graph API, deprecating features that are no longer aligned with its goals or user needs.
Strategies Used:

- **Versioning System**: Facebook uses a clear versioning system to manage changes, allowing developers to specify the version of the API they wish to use.
- **Deprecation Notices**: Facebook includes deprecation notices in the API responses to inform developers of upcoming changes.
- **Support Channels**: Developers can access support channels for assistance during the migration process.

6. Tools for Managing API Deprecation

Several tools can assist you in managing API deprecation and sunset policies effectively.

A. API Management Platforms

1. **API Gateways**: Tools like AWS API Gateway, Apigee, and Kong provide features for versioning, monitoring, and managing API traffic. They can simplify the process of deprecating endpoints and managing traffic routing.
2. **Analytics and Monitoring Tools**: Tools like Google Analytics, New Relic, and Datadog can help you monitor API usage, detect deprecated endpoint usage, and analyze user behavior during the deprecation process.

B. Documentation Platforms

1. **Swagger/OpenAPI**: Use Swagger or OpenAPI Specification to document versioning and deprecation information directly alongside your API endpoints.
2. **Postman**: Postman collections can be used to document versions and changes effectively, allowing for easy access to migration guides.

C. Communication Tools

1. **Email Automation**: Use email automation tools (e.g., Mailchimp, SendGrid) to notify users of upcoming deprecations and changes to the API.
2. **Feedback Collection**: Use tools like Typeform or SurveyMonkey to gather feedback from users regarding the deprecation process.

7. Conclusion

In this chapter, we explored the critical topic of managing API deprecation and implementing sunset policies. We began by discussing the importance of deprecation in the API lifecycle and the reasons for deprecating endpoints. We covered effective strategies for managing deprecation, including clear communication, migration guides, and grace periods.

We also examined best practices for communicating changes to users and implementing sunset policies, ensuring that deprecated features are phased out smoothly. Through real-world examples, we illustrated how companies have successfully navigated the deprecation process.

By adopting these strategies and practices, you can manage API deprecation effectively, minimize disruptions for your users, and maintain a positive relationship with your API consumers. In the next chapter, we will delve into the topic of API testing and monitoring, exploring best practices for ensuring the reliability and performance of your API over time. This knowledge will be essential for maintaining the long-term success of your API as it evolves to meet changing user needs.

Chapter 15: API Testing and Monitoring: Ensuring Reliability and Performance

As APIs become the backbone of modern applications, ensuring their reliability and performance through rigorous testing and monitoring is crucial. Effective testing strategies allow you to identify issues before they reach production, while robust monitoring practices help you maintain performance and respond to incidents in real time. In this chapter, we will explore the principles of API testing, different testing methodologies, monitoring strategies, and tools that can help you ensure your API remains reliable and performant.

1. The Importance of API Testing

API testing is essential to confirm that your API behaves as expected, meets performance requirements, and is secure from vulnerabilities. By implementing comprehensive testing practices, you can prevent critical issues from impacting users and ensure that your API continues to meet their needs.

A. Benefits of API Testing

1. **Identifies Bugs Early**: Rigorous testing helps catch bugs and issues before they reach production, reducing the risk of downtime or malfunctions in live applications.
2. **Ensures Compliance**: Testing ensures that your API adheres to established standards and specifications, providing assurance to users about its functionality.
3. **Improves Security**: Security testing can help identify vulnerabilities that may expose your API to attacks, allowing you to address them proactively.
4. **Enhances Performance**: Performance testing helps assess how well your API performs under various loads, ensuring that it can handle expected traffic without degradation.
5. **Facilitates Continuous Integration/Continuous Deployment (CI/CD)**: Integrating testing into your CI/CD pipeline allows you to automatically run tests whenever code changes are made, ensuring a consistent quality of your API.

2. Types of API Testing

API testing encompasses various types of tests, each focusing on different aspects of the API. Here are some common types of API testing:

A. Functional Testing

Functional testing verifies that the API performs its intended functions according to specifications. It focuses on testing the endpoints, request/response formats, and error handling.

1. **Test Cases**: Create test cases for each API endpoint, detailing the input, expected output, and any edge cases.
2. **Validation of Responses**: Ensure that the API returns the correct

status codes, headers, and data formats.

Example: Using a testing framework like pytest, you can create functional tests for your Flask API:

```python
Copy code
import pytest

@pytest.mark.parametrize("username, password, expected_status", [
    ("valid_user", "valid_password", 200),
    ("invalid_user", "wrong_password", 401),
])
def test_login(client, username, password, expected_status):
    response = client.post('/api/login', json={"username":
    username, "password": password})
    assert response.status_code == expected_status
```

B. Performance Testing

Performance testing evaluates how the API behaves under load, measuring response times, throughput, and resource usage.

1. **Load Testing**: Simulate multiple users accessing the API simultaneously to assess how it performs under peak conditions.
2. **Stress Testing**: Push the API beyond its limits to determine its breaking point and identify potential bottlenecks.
3. **Endurance Testing**: Test the API over an extended period to identify memory leaks and performance degradation.

Tools for Performance Testing:

- **Apache JMeter**: An open-source tool for load testing and performance measurement.

- **Locust**: A Python-based load testing tool that allows you to define user behavior in code.
- **Gatling**: A powerful load testing framework for web applications.

C. Security Testing

Security testing focuses on identifying vulnerabilities in the API that could be exploited by attackers.

1. **Authentication and Authorization Tests**: Ensure that only authenticated and authorized users can access specific endpoints.
2. **Input Validation**: Test for common vulnerabilities such as SQL injection, XSS, and command injection by sending malicious inputs.
3. **Rate Limiting Tests**: Verify that rate limiting mechanisms are in place to prevent abuse.

Tools for Security Testing:

- **OWASP ZAP**: An open-source security scanner for web applications.
- **Burp Suite**: A comprehensive suite for web application security testing.

D. Usability Testing

Usability testing assesses how easy it is for developers to understand and interact with the API.

1. **Documentation Review**: Ensure that the API documentation is clear, comprehensive, and up to date.
2. **User Feedback**: Gather feedback from developers who are using the API to identify areas for improvement.

3. Testing Methodologies

Different testing methodologies can be applied to API testing to ensure comprehensive coverage and effectiveness. Here are some common methodologies:

A. Test-Driven Development (TDD)

TDD is a software development approach where tests are written before the actual implementation of the code. This methodology emphasizes the importance of testing in the development process.

1. **Write Tests First**: Begin by writing tests for the desired functionality before implementing the code.
2. **Develop and Refactor**: Implement the code to pass the tests, then refactor as necessary while ensuring all tests continue to pass.
3. **Benefits**: TDD encourages better code design, improves code quality, and helps catch bugs early in the development process.

B. Behavior-Driven Development (BDD)

BDD is an extension of TDD that focuses on the behavior of the application from the end-user's perspective. It encourages collaboration between developers, testers, and stakeholders.

1. **Define User Scenarios**: Use natural language to define scenarios that describe how users will interact with the API.
2. **Automate Tests**: Automate the defined scenarios using BDD frameworks like Behave or Cucumber.

Example:

```gherkin
Copy code
Feature: User Login
  Scenario: Successful Login
    Given the user has a valid username and password
    When the user attempts to log in
    Then the response status should be 200
```

C. Continuous Testing

Continuous testing integrates automated testing into the CI/CD pipeline, allowing tests to run automatically whenever code changes are made.

1. **Automated Test Execution**: Set up automated tests to run at various stages of the development process, including during build, deployment, and after code changes.
2. **Rapid Feedback**: Continuous testing provides rapid feedback to developers, helping them identify and resolve issues quickly.
3. **Tools for Continuous Testing**: Use CI/CD tools like Jenkins, Travis CI, or GitHub Actions to automate the testing process.

4. Monitoring Your API

Monitoring is crucial for maintaining the health and performance of your API in production. By continuously monitoring your API, you can identify issues, track performance metrics, and ensure a seamless user experience.

A. Key Monitoring Metrics

1. **Response Times**: Measure how long it takes for your API to respond to requests. Track both average response times and outliers.
2. **Error Rates**: Monitor the percentage of requests that result in errors (e.g., 4xx and 5xx status codes). A sudden increase in error rates can

indicate underlying issues.

3. **Throughput**: Track the number of requests processed by your API over time. This metric helps you understand usage patterns and identify potential bottlenecks.
4. **Latency**: Measure the time it takes for requests to travel from the client to the server and back. High latency can negatively impact user experience.
5. **Resource Utilization**: Monitor CPU, memory, and disk usage to ensure your API operates within acceptable limits and can handle traffic efficiently.

B. Setting Up Monitoring Tools

Several tools can assist in monitoring the performance and health of your API. Here are some popular options:

1. **Application Performance Monitoring (APM) Tools**:

- **New Relic**: Provides real-time performance monitoring and insights into application performance.
- **Datadog**: Offers monitoring for cloud applications, including API performance metrics and logs.

1. **Logging and Analytics Tools**:

- **ELK Stack (Elasticsearch, Logstash, Kibana)**: A popular stack for centralized logging, allowing you to aggregate, search, and visualize logs from your API.
- **Splunk**: A comprehensive log management and analysis tool that can help identify issues and track API performance.

1. **Custom Dashboards**:

- Create custom dashboards using tools like Grafana to visualize key performance metrics and provide real-time insights into your API's health.

C. Implementing Alerts

1. **Set Up Alerts for Key Metrics**: Configure alerts for critical metrics (e.g., response times, error rates) to ensure timely intervention when issues arise.
2. **Define Alert Thresholds**: Establish thresholds for alerts based on historical performance data. For example, set an alert if response times exceed a specific threshold for a sustained period.
3. **Communication Channels**: Use communication tools like Slack, Microsoft Teams, or email to notify your team of alerts, ensuring rapid response to incidents.

5. Conducting API Load Testing

Load testing is essential for understanding how your API performs under different traffic conditions. By simulating various load scenarios, you can identify bottlenecks and optimize your API for scalability.

A. Planning Load Tests

1. **Define Load Scenarios**: Identify the key scenarios you want to test, such as high traffic, concurrent users, and peak load conditions.
2. **Determine Load Parameters**: Define parameters for your load tests, including the number of virtual users, request rates, and duration of the tests.
3. **Select a Testing Tool**: Choose a load testing tool that meets your needs, such as Apache JMeter, Locust, or Gatling.

B. Executing Load Tests

1. **Configure the Load Test**: Set up your chosen load testing tool to simulate the defined load scenarios.
2. **Run the Tests**: Execute the load tests while monitoring API performance metrics, such as response times and error rates.
3. **Analyze Results**: After the tests, analyze the results to identify performance bottlenecks, resource utilization, and areas for optimization.

C. Interpreting Load Test Results

1. **Identify Bottlenecks**: Look for patterns in the data that indicate performance bottlenecks, such as increased response times under load.
2. **Resource Utilization Analysis**: Assess how your API's resource utilization (CPU, memory, etc.) changes under different loads.
3. **Benchmarking**: Use the results as benchmarks for future performance testing, helping you track improvements or regressions over time.

6. Best Practices for API Testing and Monitoring

To ensure effective API testing and monitoring, consider the following best practices:

A. Comprehensive Test Coverage

1. **Automate Tests**: Automate as many tests as possible to ensure consistency and reduce manual testing overhead.
2. **Include Edge Cases**: Ensure that your tests cover edge cases and error scenarios, not just happy paths.
3. **Regularly Review and Update Tests**: As your API evolves, regularly review and update your tests to ensure they remain relevant.

B. Integrate Testing into CI/CD Pipelines

1. **Continuous Testing**: Implement continuous testing practices to automatically run tests as part of your CI/CD pipeline.
2. **Fail Fast**: Ensure that your CI/CD pipeline fails fast when tests do not pass, preventing broken code from being deployed.

C. Monitor in Real-Time

1. **Real-Time Monitoring**: Implement real-time monitoring to track API performance and user interactions continuously.
2. **Post-Deployment Monitoring**: Monitor your API closely after deployments to catch any issues that arise from new changes.

D. Encourage Feedback

1. **User Feedback Loops**: Encourage users to provide feedback on API performance and usability, helping you identify areas for improvement.
2. **Engage with Developers**: Participate in forums and developer communities to gather insights on common pain points and feature requests.

7. Conclusion

In this chapter, we explored the critical aspects of API testing and monitoring. We began by discussing the importance of testing in ensuring the reliability and performance of your API. We covered different types of testing, including functional, performance, security, and usability testing, along with methodologies such as TDD and BDD.

We also examined the importance of monitoring your API's performance in production, discussing key metrics to track and the tools available for effective monitoring. Load testing was highlighted as a crucial practice for understanding how your API performs under stress, and we provided guidance on planning and executing load tests.

By implementing these strategies and best practices, you can ensure the reliability, performance, and security of your Flask API, ultimately delivering a better experience for your users. In the next chapter, we will explore the topic of API versioning, discussing best practices for managing changes to your API while ensuring backward compatibility and minimizing disruptions for users. This knowledge will help you maintain a robust and adaptable API as it evolves over time.

Conclusion: The Future of API Development with Flask

In this comprehensive guide on serverless API development with Flask, we have explored a multitude of topics, ranging from the fundamentals of Flask to advanced techniques for optimizing, securing, and managing your APIs. As the digital landscape continues to evolve, APIs remain a critical component for enabling communication between different systems, applications, and services. Flask, with its flexibility and simplicity, serves as an excellent framework for building robust APIs, particularly in serverless architectures.

Key Takeaways from the Journey

1. The Power of Flask

Flask is a micro web framework that allows developers to build APIs quickly and efficiently. Its simplicity, combined with its vast ecosystem of extensions, makes it an ideal choice for both beginners and experienced developers. Throughout this book, we highlighted the following key features of Flask:

- **Minimalism**: Flask's lightweight design allows developers to start small and scale as needed. This is particularly useful in serverless

environments where resources may be limited.
- **Flexibility**: With Flask, developers can choose their own libraries and tools, leading to a customized development experience that fits the specific needs of their projects.
- **Community Support**: Flask has a vibrant community and a wealth of resources, including extensions, documentation, and tutorials that facilitate learning and problem-solving.

2. Embracing Serverless Architectures

The shift toward serverless architectures has transformed the way APIs are built and deployed. By leveraging serverless platforms like AWS Lambda, developers can focus on writing code without worrying about infrastructure management. This approach offers numerous advantages:

- **Scalability**: Serverless architectures automatically scale with demand, ensuring that your API can handle varying loads without manual intervention.
- **Cost-Effectiveness**: With serverless, you pay only for the compute time you consume, making it an economical choice for many applications, particularly those with unpredictable traffic patterns.
- **Faster Time to Market**: By eliminating the need to manage servers, developers can accelerate their development cycles and bring new features and updates to users more quickly.

3. Importance of Security

As APIs become increasingly integral to applications, security has emerged as a top priority. The book underscored the necessity of implementing robust security measures to protect sensitive data and maintain user trust. Key security practices include:

- **Authentication and Authorization**: Implementing secure authentica-

tion mechanisms, such as OAuth2 and JWT, ensures that only authorized users can access your API.
- **Data Validation**: Thoroughly validating and sanitizing input data helps protect against common vulnerabilities like SQL injection and XSS.
- **Monitoring and Logging**: Continuous monitoring of your API's performance and security posture allows for rapid detection of potential threats and issues.

4. *The Role of Documentation*

Comprehensive and user-friendly documentation is essential for the success of any API. This book emphasized best practices for creating effective API documentation, including:

- **Clarity and Simplicity**: Writing in clear, simple language makes it easier for developers to understand how to use your API.
- **Comprehensive Coverage**: Detailed endpoint descriptions, authentication methods, and error handling instructions are crucial for facilitating integration.
- **Use of Tools**: Utilizing tools like Swagger, Postman, and Read the Docs can streamline the documentation process and enhance the developer experience.

5. *Effective Testing and Monitoring*

The importance of rigorous testing and continuous monitoring cannot be overstated. These practices ensure that your API remains reliable and performant as it evolves. The book covered various types of testing, including:

- **Functional Testing**: Verifying that the API behaves as expected under normal conditions.
- **Performance Testing**: Assessing how the API performs under load,

identifying bottlenecks, and optimizing for scalability.
- **Security Testing**: Identifying vulnerabilities and ensuring that the API is protected against potential attacks.

Monitoring practices discussed included tracking key performance metrics, setting up alerts for critical issues, and using APM tools to gain insights into API behavior in production.

6. Managing Deprecation and Sunset Policies

As APIs evolve, deprecation of older endpoints and versions is inevitable. This book provided strategies for managing API deprecation effectively, including:

- **Clear Communication**: Keeping users informed of deprecation plans and providing migration guides to facilitate smooth transitions.
- **Grace Periods**: Allowing users time to adapt by offering a grace period during which both old and new versions coexist.
- **Structured Sunset Policies**: Implementing policies that define the process for phasing out deprecated features, ensuring a clear timeline and reducing user friction.

The Road Ahead: Trends in API Development

As we look to the future of API development, several trends are emerging that will shape the landscape:

1. Increased Focus on API Security

With the rise in cyber threats and data breaches, the focus on API security will only intensify. Developers will need to implement more advanced security measures, including enhanced authentication mechanisms, anomaly detection systems, and stricter access controls. Additionally, compliance with regulations such as GDPR and CCPA will necessitate robust data protection practices.

2. The Rise of GraphQL

GraphQL is gaining popularity as an alternative to traditional REST APIs. Its flexibility in querying allows clients to request only the data they need, reducing over-fetching and under-fetching issues. As developers increasingly seek more efficient ways to interact with APIs, GraphQL may become a standard in API development.

3. Serverless and Microservices

The serverless paradigm and microservices architecture are likely to continue their growth trajectory. APIs will increasingly be designed as independent services that can be deployed, scaled, and updated independently, leading to more modular and maintainable codebases. This shift will allow organizations to respond more quickly to changing business needs.

4. API-First Development

API-first development is a growing trend where APIs are designed and documented before the actual implementation begins. This approach facilitates better collaboration between development teams, ensures that APIs are built with user needs in mind, and allows for more efficient testing and iteration.

5. Enhanced API Monitoring and Analytics

As API usage grows, so will the need for sophisticated monitoring and analytics tools. Developers will seek deeper insights into API performance, user behavior, and error rates. Tools that offer real-time monitoring, predictive analytics, and machine learning capabilities will become essential for maintaining API health and performance.

6. Emphasis on Developer Experience

The focus on improving the developer experience will drive API design and documentation efforts. APIs that are easy to use, well-documented, and provide valuable support resources will gain a competitive advantage. Organizations will invest in resources that enhance the developer journey, from onboarding to troubleshooting.

Final Thoughts

The journey of mastering serverless API development with Flask has provided valuable insights and practical knowledge that can significantly impact your development practices. As APIs continue to play a critical role in the success of applications, the principles, strategies, and tools outlined in this book will empower you to build secure, efficient, and user-friendly APIs.

By embracing the key takeaways from this guide, you will be well-equipped to navigate the challenges of API development and take full advantage of the opportunities that lie ahead. Whether you are a beginner or an experienced developer, the insights gained here can help you create APIs that not only meet the needs of your users but also stand the test of time in an ever-evolving technological landscape.

www.ingramcontent.com/pod-product-compliance
Lightning Source LLC
Chambersburg PA
CBHW052146220526
45471CB00004B/1549